Love Marriage in Kabul: A Memoir

Love Marriage in Kabul: A Memoir

Sanaz Fotouhi

Gazebo Books
Summer Hill
2020

Gazebo Books
PO Box 375
Summer Hill
New South Wales 2130
Australia
gazebobooks.com.au

First published 2020

National Library of Australia
Cataloguing-in-Publication Entry
Author: Fotouhi, Sanaz
Love Marriage in Kabul: A Memoir
First edition
ISBN 978 0 6489011 0 5 (paperback).

The manuscript of *Love Marriage in Kabul: A Memoir* won the University of Melbourne's 2019 Peter Blazey Fellowship.

Cover photograph by the author.

Cover and interior design by Mountains Brown Press.

Prelude

I stood on the ledge of the flat roof of Hope House, watching the sun bleed behind Kabul's mountains. Light raindrops touched my face; they brought with them a musky smell, the scent of water quenching dry earth. It was familiar and soothing, something as ancient as time.

I had escaped up here to take a deep breath. I needed to think about what I was doing here: I didn't feel I knew anymore.

All day, we had been sitting in a room interviewing children. All day, boys and girls had sat in front of our camera, telling their harrowing stories, revealing how they had come to call this blue and white building home. All day, I had recorded their voices as Amin filmed them.

But filming these stories was not our reason for being in Kabul. We had come to make a film about the marriage of Abdul Fattah and Fatemeh. Abdul Fattah was one of the first boys Mahboba had saved. He was now a responsible young man of seventeen, and he worked at Hope House, a good-natured big brother to the younger children. Across the small valley lived Fatemeh. She was a shy fifteen-year-old who, in the absence of her deceased mother, was the backbone of her father's household. We had come in anticipation of their union. Yet, two weeks into our four-week trip, there was no sign of a marriage, only a string of obstacles. If Fatemeh didn't marry Abdul Fattah, her father would most likely marry her to some old man. Abdul Fattah would be heart-broken, and another girl would become a statistic in a violent and miserable marriage. I had seen what happened to girls like her.

We would also have no film, and Amin and I didn't want to go back to Australia empty-handed. That is why we had started to interview the children. We wanted to capture their voices so that if all else failed, maybe we could somehow make a film. That day, with each story, a knot had tightened in my throat. By the time Monireh, the last girl, sat down, the room was heavy with words spoken for the first time in near-whispers. I could feel them all around me. I could hardly breathe.

Now, standing on the rooftop, my stomach sank. If we actually did manage to make our film about the marriage, most of this footage, the many stories we had heard and recorded, would likely be edited out and left unseen, forever buried in a hard disk somewhere in Australia. For our last film, we had cut over eighty hours of footage to fifteen minutes. My heart was still heavy with painful and untold stories from our last trip to Afghanistan. I didn't have any more room to keep these stories locked in there too.

Then it dawned on me: I was here to do more than make a documentary. I was here to collect and recount untold stories that the film could not capture and show. I knew I had to write them.

As the sun sank behind the mountains, I breathed in and out and welcomed the new direction, and the fine rain which brought with it the aroma of water droplets on dry earth. This was a smell that had marked my childhood and also a dream, one that was still vividly etched in my memory many years after it came to me. I had searched for its meaning ever since. Perhaps it was this dream that had set everything in motion.

One night, in the summer of 1996, when I was fifteen and my mother and I had returned to Tehran from Los Angeles for the holidays, I dreamt that I was standing in an open field. The sky was ablaze and the rays of the sun gave shape to a desolate landscape. Far away, on the horizon, dim figures were running towards me. As they approached, I realised they were children. They roared like the waves of an ocean as they bolted across the barren land. At first I was thrilled, but as they neared horror replaced my excitement. They were dressed in torn clothes, some were barefoot, while others wore pink and green slippers far too big for their feet. The little ones kept falling in the thick mud and older boys and girls helped them up. Some were carrying smaller children in their arms or on their backs as they sprinted. Many held hands. They kept looking back into the darkness behind them, but they didn't stop until they reached the barbed wire that separated them from me. Now, close up, I could see them clearly. They had bloodied faces and bruised bodies. Suddenly, I could also understand what they were shouting.

'Help!'

It echoed everywhere around me.

I yelled back in terror, begging them to hurry over the fence. Some started to climb, catching their clothes and tiny bodies on the wire. I helped them down on my side. My arm caught on the metallic thorns; blood streamed from a large cut, but I was determined. One by one I helped the children jump down. It started to rain and the mud around us got deeper. No matter how many children I helped, more rushed towards me. I sat down in the mud and screamed.

I woke from the dream in a cold sweat, my heart pounding and my face wet with tears. The sun had just risen. The pigeons were cooing outside the open window. I breathed in and recognised the smell of the first drops of rain, instantly evaporating on Tehran's summer dust. This was the smell of home. I left the blanket spread on the floor, pulled aside the greying lace curtains of my grandmother's guest room and stepped barefoot onto the balcony. I leaned on the railing, looked down from the second floor at the garden of roses in full bloom, the mulberry trees and blackberry bushes, drank in the scents of earth and water. The smell of my childhood, now bonded forever to that terrible vision.

My grandfather opened the creaky green iron gate to the walled garden and walked in with fresh loaves of bread, slowly making his way across. He didn't look up, but floated silently below me and out of view, into the house. I stood there thinking about the dream, to the music of the birds.

Then, I hadn't known what to make of the dream. I wrote it down in detail in my teenage diary, and for years thought about it often. Now, on the roof of Hope House, a safe house for children and widows, I thought perhaps the dream was much older than me, set in motion by events that took place long before I was born.

The story, as far as I know, began with my grandfather's decision against all odds to give my father an education. My grandfather was a dreamer, and had some ideas larger than his time. This was one of them. My father, the eldest of ten, was born in 1941, on the cusp of Iran's shift from the feudal system. They lived in Jahizdan, a village of less than one hundred households, in north-west Iran. At that time, the boys were sent to work on the fields as soon as they could walk. Often, after a day's work, they were rounded up by the village chief and given wooden guns to practise army drills. Back then, there was no school in Jahizdan and no one really saw the value of education as it took the children away from the workforce. That is why my grandfather, along with a few others from surrounding villages, started their own *maktab*, run by the only person in the area literate enough to teach. The teacher lived two villages away, three hours' walk through the mountains each way. He would trudge up the slopes and through the snow on a donkey once a week and lodge at the houses of privileged students, who usually had a spare room in which classes could be held. There, they would sit and recite the alphabet and practise writing on the dust floor.

While this was more than enough for the other parents, my grandfather continued to dream of his son one day becoming the village *mullah*. To fund this dream, he launched into a business venture.

One summer morning in the early 1950s, as

everyone in the village watched with their mouths wide open, a dilapidated truck huffed through the rough terrain to his orchard. Onlookers thought he had lost his mind and stood around in amusement as he chopped down some of the apricot trees with the driver, loading them onto the back of the truck. The children, including my father, who used to climb the trees and eat from their fruit asked him what he was doing.

'I am selling these trees to matchstick factories in Tabriz,' he said, wiping down the sweat on his brow.

'But why?' my father asked.

'To pay for you to study.' There was the beginning of my father's future: on the back of a truck heading to Tabriz.

Five years and thousands of matchsticks later, father and son finally took the first step together towards this dream. On a chilly autumn day, with a bundle of bedding tied up in a huge sheet with a big knot, and a bread roll with cheese, my father boarded the truck with his father. As the other children watched, my father, sitting in a motorised vehicle for the first time, and nauseous from the lurching of the truck around the bends, began his journey towards education.

He didn't know that this road would take him not only to Tabriz but also halfway across the world, thanks to a coincidence that would introduce him to the English language and eventually change the fate of our family and lineage.

Now, on the roof of Hope House, in the rain, remembering these stories, I felt thankful. These were my roots, in the earth, in the dust and the mud. They made me feel strong. The story that my grandfather had begun had led me here: this is where I had to be, and this was the work I had to do. I had to tell the stories that were here, all around me.

Part I

1

Despite faith and prayer and a surprisingly smooth transit, a strange nervousness took over me as we neared Kabul. My stomach was turning. I looked out of the plane window as we started to descend.

Kabul is like a bowl, a plateau surrounded by majestic snow-capped mountains. Having flown over the teeming landscape of Tehran, which over the last decade or so had mushroomed beyond its capacity, I noticed the clear shape of this city. The wide roads and separated suburbs spoke of the legacy of the pre-war promise of urban planning. But as the plane descended further, that structure was revealed to be a shell-shocked skeleton: bones with nothing left to offer.

I wondered if we were going to be offered anything or offer anything back. I held Amin's hand, hoping that we had made the right decision.

The night before we left Tehran for Kabul, my father had sat us down for a chat. He told us that in his heart he felt that our intention should be to make this trip for the sake of the orphans and the widows we would encounter. He felt that if we had this intention we would be guided by divine forces to have a successful project. 'Put aside your own personal gains and get out of your own way,' he said. 'Allow yourselves to be a medium for their voices to reach the world.' His words clenched my heart.

I left Tehran with a deep sense of responsibility.

Like the few other passengers travelling from Tehran to Kabul, we had to transit in the ancient city of Mashhad on the only weekly flight, Friday afternoon. We'd decided to stay there for a night. I am not a religious person but I felt that it would be auspicious to start a trip to Afghanistan among hundreds of thousands of pilgrims and spiritual seekers; even before it had begun, this trip had already been the cause of so much unease.

That night, I sat for hours in the mirrored halls of the shrine of Imam Reza, to whom people prayed to make their wishes come true. Among the seekers, wrapped in a compulsory borrowed white chador, surrounded by the scent of rose water and the sounds of pigeons, I opened my heart and sought divine intervention.

Walking along the runway tarmac now, welcomed by a huge billboard of Afghan freedom fighter Ahmad Shah Massoud, our every move watched by men with rifles, we knew there was no going back. I took a deep breath of Kabul's cool March air, and followed the guard into the arrivals hall.

We lined up to have our passports checked. Amin was edgy, particularly irritated by a man behind us wearing a Pashtun hat, pushing us to go ahead when the officer had not asked us to step forward.

'Next,' said the clean-shaven, blond and green-eyed visa officer inside a glassed cubicle. Amin and I both moved forward. He took Amin's Iranian passport first and flipped through it. He looked at the visa, then again at the picture. 'This is not you,' he said in Dari.

'Of course it's me,' Amin replied with an odd laugh.

'It doesn't look like you.'

He examined the picture again and looked at Amin. The passport picture was more than ten years old. It showed a young man on the cusp of puberty. Amin, fully bearded, looked nothing like the teenager in the photo. When the passport had expired after ten years, the Iranian embassy in Canberra had accidentally renewed it instead of issuing a new one. I always knew this would cause trouble one day.

The visa officer continued to scrutinise the passport, flipping through the pages, feeling them under his fingers. Beads of sweat were forming on Amin's face. We said nothing. The man left the cubicle, and after what felt like a long wait returned with an older officer.

'Is this you?' The other man, with a two-day beard and a bit of weight around his belly, looked at the photo and then at Amin.

'Yes, it is me.' He explained what happened at the embassy. The man flipped through the passport and saw that Amin had two other Afghan visas. 'So you have been here before.'

'Yes.'

'You're a journalist?'

Mahboba had instructed us emphatically to avoid saying we were journalists or filmmakers. They had been targeted by terrorist groups. But the previous visa in Amin's passport was a journalist one.

'No,' he said as he paused, thinking of what to say next. 'This time I am only visiting an orphanage to make some reports for them.' Then he added, 'I am here with my wife. She will help me.' He pulled me in closer.

'Which orphanage?' the older officer asked.

'Sister Mahboba Rawi's Hope House.'

'Okay. I want to believe you. It is my duty to do this. But it doesn't look like you.' He kept glancing back at Amin and the photo.

Then he left and took the passport with him. We waited for what felt like another eternity. People behind us were becoming agitated. This was the only line operating and we were holding everyone up.

Finally the man came back. 'Do you have any other form of identification, from Iran, maybe?'

'Yes, sure.' Amin rummaged in his bag and pulled out his Iranian birth certificate, which coincidentally bore the same photo.

'Brother, why didn't you show me this sooner?' said the man with a smile. Amin shrugged.

A relieving stamp on the page. 'Get your passport changed, brother. You will get yourself in trouble,' he said as we walked through, leaving a line of frustrated people behind.

2

My father had turned out to be a star student, with a gift for languages. His excellent academic work at Tabriz secured him a place in Iran's biggest Islamic university, in Qum, funded still by apricot matchsticks. But when he reached Qum, far from the familiar landscape of his childhood, there was a new challenge. In Tabriz, classes catered for the local students and were taught in Azari. In Qum, they were taught in Farsi, as well as Arabic. At eighteen, my father was exposed to Iran's national language for the first time. His wealthy city peers mocked his provincial accent, but instead of taking this to heart my father devoted himself to mastering Farsi. Within a few months his accent was indistinguishable from that of others.

One afternoon, chatting with some of his new-found friends near the library, my father spotted a small book in one of their hands. The characters on it reminded him of the signs on the old jute bags they used for carrying grains during harvest season in the village.

'What is that?' he enquired.

'It is a guide for dayere cat mitod,' his friend replied.

'What is dayere cat mitod?'

'It is a book for learning Englisi.'

Intrigued, he wanted to know what Englisi was. He rushed to the campus bookstore, a dingy hole in the wall for theology texts. He eagerly picked one and paid the 20 rials, a good amount of money which could have bought him a number of basic necessities. As he was leaving, the shopkeeper called out, 'Young man, you should know that this is only a guidebook for the English text taught in the high schools. If you want to make use of it, you must have the English text itself as well.' My father paid another 15 rials for the other book and ran to his room to explore them.

He became obsessed. He locked himself in his room and practised under candlelight at night instead of enjoying the occasional stroll down the streets of Qum with his friends. Between the textbook and the guide, he managed to voice the words from the Farsi transcript and understand the first few lessons.

One afternoon in the bazaar, he came across a man listening to sounds on the radio no one seemed to understand. 'What is that?' my father asked.

'It is the BBC radio,' the man said.

'Do you understand what it says?'

'No, but I like the sound of it. I would like to learn English one day.'

'Is that English? Is that what English sounds like?' The answer sent my father in search of a battery-operated radio. He brought it back to the man to tune it to the BBC. From then on, he lay in the dark in his room until late every night, repeating the sounds he heard.

His secret spilled out with the strange noises coming through his room as the other boys lined up behind his door, laughing and wondering what he was doing. They would talk gibberish whenever they saw him on campus, asking if he could understand what they were saying. He became a laughing stock, until one of the boys who had some years of high school and knew some English offered to help him. Ignoring the bullying, gradually and painstakingly my father learned enough to realise that the title of the little book which had introduced him to English was Direct Method, not 'dayere cat mitod'.

He was now confident enough to say that he could speak English, and started to teach it to his peers, some of whom had begun by then to see its thrill.

Although my father had started in Qum with the hope of becoming a cleric, fate and his new-found language expanded his world, steering him away from the path of spiritual leadership. After leaving Qum in the late 1960s, he was recruited by Bank Melli, Iran's first national bank, as a clerk.

In the early 1970s, Iran was a prospering country with a promising future and an elegant capital city, and had good relations with America and the rest of the world. Many Iranian companies were sending their brightest employees to train abroad. In 1976, having achieved the highest score in a national English test, my father was sent by Bank Melli to New York for two years, together with my mother, and my seven-year-old sister Sara. They returned to Iran just before the 1978 upheavals that led to the Islamic Revolution. My father continued working at the bank and got promoted to the foreign affairs section.

Fourteen years later, when I was eleven, after the ceasefire of the war between Iran and Iraq, and a few months after Sara was married, my father was once again chosen to travel overseas, this time as the chief executive officer for Bank Melli's Tokyo office. This was the first of a string of posts that would take us from Tokyo to New York, Los Angeles and finally Hong Kong almost a decade later. It was after he had retired that he was approached, in 2002, to go to Kabul to start a joint bank between Iran and Afghanistan.

Amin and I first visited my father in Afghanistan in early 2006. The things we saw and heard had intrigued us, and we came back in July the same year for a longer visit, with the idea of making a film. The footage we recorded became a short documentary called *Hidden Generation*. It investigated why, after the fall of the Taliban, an increasing number of women were trying to commit suicide by setting themselves on fire. The documentary became the highlight of Amin's career as a young filmmaker. Along with plans to make a related feature film, it got him into the Australian Film, Television and Radio School. At that time, only four applicants were accepted in each field every year out of hundreds, and Amin was one of them.

We moved to Sydney and rented a unit near the school. I was excited about Sydney. I had moved to Canberra from Hong Kong after meeting Amin. Leaving behind a twenty-four-hour city, for the first few days I had thought the Canberrans were on public holidays and everyone had left town. Apparently it was the busiest time of the year. The move to Sydney felt like it would be a breath of fresh air.

By this time, Amin was trying to get funding to make a feature film on the back of *Hidden Generation*. Initially, the idea was to return to Afghanistan to find, follow and film some of the surviving women. The fifteen-minute film we had ended up with showed only glimpses.

But to explore the situation more deeply, we had

to do it in a more accessible way. People who had seen the film told us how hard it was to sit through it without turning away or even walking out. The confronting content that was still haunting me also made it hard for our audience to engage. I could see this now. We needed to make something more gentle, with a way in for the viewer. And to do that, we needed to find a story, perhaps one that was different from what the short film had covered. I took time out to research this alongside my PhD. But months of work only led to a number of dead ends.

One lead had seemed promising. It took us to an Afghan woman who had migrated to Australia after a difficult life in Afghanistan and it turned out that she wanted to work with someone who would highlight the perils of Islam for women. I politely declined. *Hidden Generation* investigated the reasons why more and more women in Afghanistan were burning themselves as a form of suicide, and one of the purposes of the film had been to show that Islam in itself was not the culprit. It was, ironically, only after the fall of the Taliban, the strictest Islamic regime on earth, that women's self-immolation had risen. After talking to all kinds of people, including doctors, nurses, social workers, religious people, people on the streets, and the victims and their families, it seemed the cause was a convergence of cultural and historical elements, with Islamic extremism being just one of many factors. I knew that if we chose to show a single factor – Islam – as the main reason women were burning themselves by the hundreds, we would have a story that many were ready to hear. But that was not the story we wanted to tell.

The futile search for a topic we could develop into a feature film was taking its toll on me. The making of *Hidden Generation* had changed my life profoundly. I had borne witness to the great suffering of women and I had done a good job hiding my trauma. But back in Australia I felt helpless. I felt the only way to move forward was to show the world what was happening to women in Afghanistan.

Adding to the burden of pain and responsibility was the accidental loss of all of my photos from that trip, including those of the women I had met, in a hard-drive failure. When I discovered the damage one night, I fell into an uncontrollable and maddening grief. Weeks of melancholy followed. In my head, over and over again, I tried to remember all the details of their faces, so that I could at least write about the women I had met.

I lived in a void the first year back from Kabul. I couldn't even talk about how I felt and what I had seen; people only wanted to know so much before they stepped out of the conversation. Everyone was busy with things that looked inane to me. Compared to what I had seen in Afghanistan, their worries seemed unjustified and meaningless and my comments about other people living in far worse conditions only widened the chasm.

I became unable to buy anything for myself. Clothes, shoes and accessories, things I had liked and spent good money on before, now seemed expensive and worthless. I decided to dedicate myself to my PhD, but I couldn't concentrate. What I was producing didn't matter in the larger scheme of things, where people were dying and being killed. My supervisor's smallest criticism reinforced the futility of my pursuit. I saw myself, at twenty-six, as an aging woman with nothing to contribute to the world.

The loneliness of being in a new city pushed me into a cave, and the burnt women of Kabul haunted its entrance. Writing a thesis became a way for me to dig myself out. Every morning after Amin left for his classes, I forced myself out of bed. But alone, with no access to resources or colleagues, I felt that I was digging all day to end up at night where I had started. Amin was gone all the time, building a social and professional network. My life was reduced to a computer screen. Making friends with Amin's circle wasn't helpful and the encounters were always awkward. I stopped going out with them, even when he insisted. I sat at home alone on Friday and Saturday nights, desperately trying to find my way. I tried to write poetry and short stories about Afghanistan to find a way out through them. They led nowhere. I always ended where I started, sometimes even deeper in.

After months of this, I still felt the pain but I also began to feel distant from the things that had once passionately moved me. When I watched *Hidden Generation*, I didn't cry any more. I had lost my connection with the women whose anguish I had witnessed. I was helpless and full of guilt. Slowly, I came to understand that I was in a spiritual crisis.

Then, in 2007, someone I knew asked me if I had heard of Mahboba Rawi, an Afghan-Australian woman who ran a charity organisation from Sydney called Mahboba's Promise. It was a lead that seemed slightly promising.

I called that afternoon, and Mahboba herself picked up the phone. I introduced myself and Amin as Iranian filmmakers living in Sydney. She asked me why I was not speaking Farsi, so I switched and she seemed more comfortable.

When I told Mahboba that we had made a film on women's self-immolation, she responded, like the people at the Afghan embassy in Canberra, that she had never heard of such an issue. Then she began to question me: who were we, who did we work for and what did we want to achieve? I heard scepticism in her tone. Mahboba finally said there had been many people interested in making films with and about her, but she didn't want to be involved in projects that reiterated certain images of Afghanistan. I assured her that we had the same aim and with that her tone changed. I asked if she had any interesting stories that could lead to potential documentaries; she said she had much more than we could ever imagine.

I googled Mahboba after I hung up. I learned that Mahboba had escaped Afghanistan as a teenager during the Russian invasion and migrated to Australia, where, years later, she had set up Mahboba's Promise. She had built several orphanages across Afghanistan and been the agent for educating hundreds of girls in rural areas. Hope House, a centre that housed about a hundred children, was her biggest achievement then. For her efforts Mahboba was listed as one of 'fifty Australians who matter' by *The Age* in 2005. I then arranged a meeting with her.

We arrived at a townhouse with sheets hanging to dry at the front and shoes lined up at the door, and I knew immediately we had come to the right place. I had seen photos of Mahboba; she had dark skin and intense eyes and was always covered with a scarf. In reality she was less intense, and gentle in demeanour. She greeted us wearing a large white shawl around her that covered half her body and flew over her skirt.

Mahboba's place was scarcely furnished, like a house in Kabul, with only a two-seater sofa and a small coffee table. Mahboba directed us to the sofa. She sat across from us on the floor, leaning against some cushions, next to a huge vase with long-stemmed plastic flowers. I had seen a picture of her in the same spot on a website but had not thought it was her Sydney house.

Mahboba didn't offer us anything to eat or drink because it was Ramadan. Whatever was simmering on the stove, for the evening meal, smelled good. She greeted us kindly and talked about her various projects including Hope House and a school in Panjshir which was supported by a girls' high school in Sydney. She talked about many different things but none in detail, so it was hard to fathom the extent of her work.

When we talked about *Hidden Generation* Mahboba didn't seem concerned about what it depicted. Her first question was about those who burned themselves and survived. Survival was worse than death for some of these women. Not only were most of them physically deformed for the rest of their lives, but they had to face a shameful return home.

Eventually, Mahboba told us that several years before, an Australian film crew had been interested in making a film about her work in Afghanistan. A team had been prepared and the tickets purchased. A short time before the team was due to travel Mahboba had seen another program by them, and thought it was biased. Despite all the preparations, she had cancelled the project. She was giving us a warning, and relieving herself of any guarantee of cooperation unless the project was to her liking. This was a woman who knew exactly what she wanted.

Mahboba then said she would show us the office out of which hundreds of orphans and widows were supported. I expected us to drive somewhere, but it was in her garage, tiled and furnished with four desks, shelving and filing cabinets overflowing with documents. A young woman with curly hair was working at the only computer.

'Everything that has ever been done,' Mahboba told us, 'has happened from this garage.' In the glossy promotional material, Mahboba's Promise looked just like any large-scale charity. But in reality it was a more modest affair, passing donations directly to the sponsored, without taking a cut to sustain the organisation. It only had one paid staff member and a dedicated group of volunteers across Australia.

Mahboba pushed through the overflowing room to the back and brought a copy of her memoir, *Mahboba's Promise*. The blue cover had her standing among a group of children, a loving mother gazing down. She explained how the book helped promote the organisation as she handed the copy to me. She must have felt my curiosity, because she added, 'This book will also tell you about my life.'

Before we said our goodbyes, Mahboba hugged me and said she had a good feeling about working with a young Iranian couple like us. We shared a similar cultural background and understood each other's needs. Mahboba grabbed a bunch of flyers, just as we were about to head out, and told us to pass them on to our friends.

3

In March 2009, two years after our first encounter with Mahboba in Sydney, we finally made it to Kabul.

At the arrivals hall people dissipated into the dark room where a luggage conveyor belt creaked and struggled, presenting the oversized suitcases borne from the belly of our plane. In their ugliness, they were the bundles that carried all the hope and livelihood of returning refugees, things they needed to start their new lives now that their unwelcome stay in Iran was over. As we watched men sorrowfully hurling heavy bags, I was glad we had decided to travel light.

Then I became aware of our difference. Dressed in the dowdiest and most shapeless overcoat that I could borrow from my mother, and wearing a tight skullcap under my scarf to keep my hair back, I no longer looked like an uptown Tehrani girl. I thought I would blend in with the Afghan women who wore the even more shapeless chador on our plane. But with our clean carry-on luggage with intact wheels, and several camera bags, we stood out among the cartfuls of oversized, roped and torn suitcases.

When I had gone to the Afghan embassy in Tehran to organise our visas a couple of weeks before, though it was early in the morning, there had been hundreds of people, mostly Afghans, lined up all the way down the street, waiting, sitting in clusters, looking bored or worried. I was one of very few Iranians in the crowd, and one of the even fewer women. Dressed in a blue jacket that came above my knees, three-quarter sleeves, skinny jeans, Gucci sunglasses and a scarf partially covering my hair, I was obviously out of place beside the few chador-clad women who were sitting in the corners waiting for their men. They were staring at me inquisitively. I had quickly fixed myself up, pulling down my sleeves as much as possible, putting away my sunglasses, and yanking my scarf forward to hide the strands of my hair. But it was the eve of Nou Rouz, the Persian New Year, and we had only a few days to get our papers sorted before we were due in Kabul, so I had ignored the stares, and pushed my way to the front.

Now, too, I felt out of place but we self-consciously pushed our way through the crowd. We trotted around looking for Mahboba's brother Seddiq. We had never met him and had no idea what he looked like. Nonetheless, we walked into the bright entrance of the airport arrivals, waiting for someone to approach us. But quickly, the small hall emptied as the last men and women pushed their cartfuls of bags out and left through the glass doors. Within minutes, Amin and I were the only passengers standing in the terminal, being observed suspiciously by immigration officers, shopkeepers and the men with rifles.

We decided to sit and wait. Our plane had landed on time, at twelve-thirty. For the first half-hour, I wasn't worried. Given the road conditions in Kabul, perhaps Seddiq was in traffic.

I distracted myself by observing the airport.

The biggest change was the lack of US military

presence. On our last trip, there had been a fortified base at the entrance, staffed by armed men in uniform, wearing helmets and bullet-proof vests; it had really felt like a war zone. In its place now stood a security stall covered by a green and white advertisement promoting women's education, sponsored by a phone company. The ad in Dari read, 'A healthy society equals healthy and educated women'.

Women, it seemed, had also replaced the American soldiers, as a number of female officers patrolled the airport in their deep-grey uniform of long skirts, shapeless jackets and loosely worn black scarves. They nodded and smiled at me, one of the few female passengers in the airport, and I greeted them back.

Forty-five minutes passed and still no sign of Seddiq. Had he been given the wrong date? Amin assured me that in their last email exchange he had double-checked the time and date.

'Buy a SIM card from the shop and call him,' I suggested.

Amin went to a little shop selling expensive imported snacks and drinks from Iran as I waited.

He came back quickly.

'I don't have his number.'

'What do you mean you don't have his number?' I asked in disbelief.

'The only number I have is his Australian one.' Seddiq, like Mahboba, divided his time between Kabul and Sydney.

'Why didn't you think of this? How could you not get his number?' I sat down.

There was no point arguing now.

The shopkeeper, watching this exchange, suggested we take a taxi. But, rummaging through our notes, we discovered that we didn't have an address for our destination either. I stood up, my head pounding, and I breathed through the moment.

Amin suggested we contact Mahboba in Sydney and get Seddiq's number in Kabul. As he walked off to do that, I sat down again, feeling faint.

How naïve could I be? We were going into a war zone, and I had based our trip on faith and a prayer that all would be well. What would happen if we couldn't get in touch with anyone?

The whole trip suddenly seemed unplanned and unstructured. We only had a vague idea about filming the story of a marriage at an orphanage – and we didn't even know exactly where that was, and whether the marriage would happen. What if it didn't work out? And what if Mahboba, who was to arrive from Sydney in two days' time, didn't bring the camera and equipment? What if she didn't come at all? How would our safety be assured? What if one of us was hurt or even killed?

Up to then, I had convinced myself and everyone around me, including my parents, that the trip would follow a perfectly sound and logical idea. But now the whole enterprise seemed illogical, irresponsible, even dangerous.

4

Before departing for Kabul we had spent nearly three months with my parents in their three-bedroom apartment in Tehran. During that time, as we mapped out our journey, I also mapped the worries on my parents' faces.

In the early days of our stay, my parents had not taken our decision to go back to Kabul seriously, just as nobody in 2002 had initially taken my father's idea to go to Kabul seriously.

When my father retired in 2001, my parents had chosen to return to Iran. They had missed much of their two grandchildren's childhood. They settled in a comfortable apartment in a leafy complex in

Shahrak-e Gharb, one of Tehran's quiet suburbs, once known for its wide streets and now for its trendy shopping malls. My father occupied himself by writing his memoir and catching up on years of reading, while my mother spent time with my sister and her children and, with my encouragement, studied to become a yoga teacher. They lived the life of a retired couple, winding down after all the hard work.

Or so we thought, until my father received a call asking if he would be interested to help set up Aryan Bank in Kabul, a new entity which was to be a joint venture between an Iranian bank and an Afghan one. They wanted him to oversee the process and manage the branch in Kabul.

2002 Kabul, however, was one of the most dangerous places on earth. The Taliban had been ruling the country since 1995. By the time they were ousted by the Americans in 2001, Afghanistan was in ruins, a country lacking any real infrastructure to carry it into the new era. Foreign countries and businesses immediately saw both its needs and potential. But with ongoing hostilities between the Taliban and various other forces, in 2002 the country was violent and unstable. Particular targets were foreigners and their new businesses, like the one my father was to establish.

Despite this real danger, my father was keen to take the post. He saw it as his contribution to building the future of Afghanistan. Everyone else thought he was mad. Family members ridiculed him. His friends laughed at him. My mother threatened to leave. My sister stopped talking to him.

But I encouraged him. Perhaps if I were asked for advice today, I would be afraid for my father's safety and tell him not to go. At that time all I had was support. I knew he thrived on work, and to deny him such an opportunity would be selfish of us. My father had aged since his retirement and I saw this project as rejuvenating. I was young; I felt he would be safe. And he felt he would be okay too. So he took the job.

His dedication was admirable. It was this decision that eventually brought Afghanistan to my attention. It created an opening I could step through to create my own relationships and make my own small contribution to the country and its people.

Amin and I faced a similar wall of worries from my family when we announced that we were going back to make another film. The idea was wrapped in silence, but then it slowly and painfully unravelled as plans solidified and a departure date was announced. The tension built up and the silence gradually gave way to single words, statements, conversations and bloomed into full arguments.

The main concern was for our safety.

We were heading to Kabul in the lead up to the 2009 presidential elections. My parents were following the news on CNN and BBC and not a day went by when Afghanistan was not mentioned for some gruesome suicide bombing or attack.

During all this, I got caught in the web of my mother's worry.

It usually began with small statements, something like 'Afghanistan seems so dangerous these days,' to which I would respond with some random statement to avoid conversation. Then the ignored words would change shape into casual dialogues struck up in the unlikeliest places, like when the two of us were driving to go grocery shopping.

'Do you know, a few days ago, I heard on the radio

about this orphanage near Tabriz.' She was trying to keep me in Iran by stealth. 'They encourage the kids to become teachers in the same school. And then some of them marry each other. So they understand each other's pain.' After a pause she cautiously got to her point. 'So, you know, that's a great topic for a film you could make. Do you want to look into it? Instead of going to Afghanistan…'

'Maman, we have made a decision to go. People are waiting for us there. People are waiting for this film in Australia.'

'So it is confirmed.'

'For the twentieth time, Maman, it is confirmed.'

'Do you have to go too? Can't Amin go by himself?'

'Are you serious?'

'I don't see why you need to go.'

'It is my responsibility, I made a promise and I want to go.'

'Can't you get someone to replace you?'

We built webs like this every day. I would walk away, trying to disentangle myself, but find I was still tangled, because then she wouldn't talk to me the whole day, even when I approached her about other things.

One night at dinner, Amin and I were talking about some friends who had just gone to Europe. My mother put a dish on the table more heavily than usual, then shuffled and pushed cutlery around in the drawers. When a cupboard was slammed, I knew something was wrong. I kept silent.

'What's going on?' my father asked.

'Nothing,' she said as she almost threw the plates on the table and turned her back to us. My father looked at us and queried with a hand gesture.

'What's wrong, Maman Jan?' I asked.

'Amin…' she turned around with red eyes, and said very firmly, 'why do you think you can take my daughter to a war zone? What gives you the right to convince her to do such dangerous things? Do you think we found her under a bush?'

Amin was choked into silence. I opened my mouth to say something but my father began instead, 'I don't think…'

'You…you out of everyone, do not talk!' she shouted, turning to him. 'You are the culprit in all this trouble. If you had not gone, then none of this would have happened. You opened the floodgates and now I have to deal with all of this.' We sat in awe as she continued, 'Now, Amin...tell me.'

'Umm...' Amin cleared his throat and began very politely. 'Please understand that I didn't make her do anything. Sanaz has chosen to go because she has taken on a responsibility.'

'A responsibility that you and her father put on her,' she responded.

'Maman, please,' I intervened.

'You...you don't talk either. You don't even care about how I feel.' She turned around pointing a finger. 'You don't ever listen to me and don't let me talk to get things off my chest.' She broke down, tears streaming down her face. 'I am a human being too. Why do I have to stay awake every night until four thinking about what might happen to you two? None of you listen to me or want to hear what my concern is.'

'I am sorry,' I said.

'See...people go to Europe on holidays, and my child, she has to go to Afghanistan and roll around in the mud.'

'I have already been to Europe,' I said. 'I want to go to Afghanistan.'

'I am not talking to you. Do not talk to me. I am talking to Amin.'

Amin teared up. 'I am sorry, I don't know what to say. I really didn't know how you were feeling about this. Why didn't you tell us sooner?'

'She shuts me out,' she said, again pointing to me, 'and he doesn't even care,' my mother continued, turning her head towards my father.

'Talk to me, then,' Amin said. 'What is on your mind?'

And then my mother spilled out all her concerns about danger, food, disease, and being caught up in some suicide bombing incident. We all sat there, for the first time, listening to her. When she was finished, Amin said, 'I am sorry you feel like this. I really don't know what to do or say to make you feel better.'

'Don't take her with you,' my mother replied without missing a beat.

'Maman…it's not about him. It is my choice,' I said, enraged. I left the table, went to our room and crawled under the sheets.

Who were we kidding? All of us, especially my father, knew the danger we were facing in choosing to go back.

5

In 2006, when Amin and I visited my father in Kabul, we stayed at the Intercontinental. At that time it was a safe haven for the oddest assortment of expats, journalists, bankers, NGO workers, and others on mysterious business. It promised security and provided such luxuries as clean sheets, running water, hot showers, and generators that kicked in quickly when the electricity failed, which it did, several times a day.

The false sense of security this gave us on our first trip had made us ill-prepared for what we'd face when we left the safety of the hotel.

One hot July night, Kazem, our driver, insisted on taking us out to dinner. We had never eaten out in Afghanistan. Our first concern, of course, was the safety of the food. Kazem assured us that the place he had in mind served so much food that any fresh meat they cut in the morning would be finished that night. Testament to this was a crowd lining up outside the restaurant as a man frantically fanned skewers of fresh meat on a charcoal barbecue, just keeping up with demand.

The interior of this little restaurant was a surprise.

The Taliban had almost completely eradicated the female presence in public: under their reign, among other things, unaccompanied women were not allowed to leave their houses, women's images were not to be represented in any way in public, and the depiction of female celebrities was strictly forbidden and punishable. After the Taliban, women gained the right to appear in public, but the image of the unveiled woman was still something not publicly presented. Female faces only appeared on signboards for bridal and hair salons; these were painted generically, and didn't show any identifiable individual.

But in this restaurant, like the inside of many rickshaws we later saw in the city of Herat and in other restaurants we dared to try, the walls were plastered with images of unveiled women, especially of the blue-eyed, fair-skinned Indian beauty Aishwarya Rai, reflecting the Afghan obsession with Bollywood. Here, in a small space plastered wall to wall, floor to ceiling with Aishwarya's seductive face, we sat next to stout old men, their plump wives half-covered in burqas and their children, and young men from provinces, eating greasy *chapali kabab* with our hands.

I was seduced, not by the actress's gaze, but by a milky beauty in a cup, offered by an overweight man with beads of sweat forming on his upper lip in the July heat. I should have thought twice about how often the electricity would have failed that day. I chose the ice cream instead of tea.

The next morning, I woke up with my stomach turning. I skipped the buffet. The visible smog of the day added a low-frequency headache I carried with me out of the hotel. We set out to explore the famous Koocheh Morgha, or Chicken Street, an ancient lane where chicken vendors used to sell their animals, which had gradually turned into the capital's centre for sometimes-dubious antiques and crafts. Shop after shop, floor to ceiling, was piled with metal carvings, woodwork, silverware, traditional clothes, shawls, ancient carpets and other odd objects. But I couldn't focus on looking for hidden treasures. The musky smell of the shops was making me sick. I had to run out for some fresh air, but only got as far the open gutter nearly overflowing with murky water and junk, where I sat down. Amin rushed out to help me. Onlookers crowded around as Amin tried to balance his camera, hold my hand and take me to the car. I was dripping with cold sweat. I couldn't respond to Amin's questions.

I realised then that I had not packed any medication. We drove away, with my eyes closed and head spinning. When Kazem stopped at a pharmacy, I wanted to say I didn't want to take any medication, but I was too sick to speak. He and Amin came back with two sheets of pills, which I examined with half closed eyes – made in Pakistan – hoping they were at least not expired. Repeating the pharmacist's instructions, Amin told me to take one of each. One was for vomiting and the other, a tranquilliser of some sort. Despite resisting, I was forced to take them and was driven back to the hotel. They knocked me out instantly. At the Intercontinental, I could hardly stand in the elevator as it travelled the two floors up. I stumbled into the room like a drunk and collapsed on the bed.

When I woke up, it was pitch black. The only thing visible was the huge green numbers of the digital clock reading nine-thirty. It took me a few minutes to feel my body and realise where I was and that Amin was not there. I called him and then Kazem. They didn't pick up. I felt a pinch in my heart. Every night so far in Kabul we had been safely in our hotel room by nine o'clock, writing, watching television, or even sleeping. There was nothing else, at least that we knew of, to do in Kabul after sunset.

I was still in and out of the dream world. I lay back and turned on the TV. After one round of channel-hopping, I called them again. Still no response. Should I call the hotel management? Someone in Iran?

I waited. With eyes half-open, I let my mind rest on the images on the TV screen. I must have fallen asleep because I woke up to the sound of the phone nearly two hours later. It was Amin.

'Where have you been?' I asked, barely able to speak.

'In jail,' he responded.

'In jail?' I echoed, thinking he was joking, making up an excuse because they had gone somewhere fun. He said he would explain when he got back.

After dropping me off, Amin had returned to the Aina Media Centre, which had become our working base. There, he had recognised the actor Bibi from her role as the loving grandmother in Seddiq Barmak's 2003 film *Osama*. The award-winning film tells the story of a little girl in Taliban-occupied Afghanistan who is forced to dress as a boy to work and bring in income for her impoverished family.

Bibi had used her income from this role to take care of her own family, her grandchildren, and some of her neighbourhood's orphans. Since *Osama* she had been cast for small roles, and that day Bibi had travelled to Aina to see if there was anything else coming up. When she wanted to return home, Amin had suggested they could drop her off and interview her at her house on their way back.

They stopped in front of a large apartment block, its walls drilled with bullet holes. From the outside, it looked like any bombed-out block in Kabul. Inside, the apartments were just shells. They had been targeted when half-built, and eventually the damage had been so bad that they were abandoned by the investors. With only a cement structure on each floor and some rough walls dividing up what had once promised to become luxurious apartments, they still served a purpose. They were occupied by hundreds of families, who could never have afforded to live in these buildings had they been finished. In the absence of interior structures, each family had put up rugs and curtains to mark their homes, and protected themselves from the elements according to their means. Some had invested in putting glass in the empty window frames, while others, who saw this abode as temporary, had covered theirs with thick plastic. Children swarmed the building, running in the dark bullet-riddled staircases, up and down the many rail-less stairs. There was no electricity, running water, plumbing or toilets.

Bibi, whose face had been seen by comfortable and tearful audiences in cinemas and on televisions around the world, shared one of the rooms with several orphans she took care of. She could live here forever, tending to the pot plants that brought some life to the dreary space, she had told Amin, but she did not want the children to do the same.

After recording an interview with Bibi, Amin and Kazem headed back to the hotel. As usual, on the way, Amin was casually filming the streets from the van. They passed a palace-like building erected next to a tent shantytown. A few blocks later, the police stopped them. They wanted to know why he had been filming the General's house.

Amin asked who the General was and which was his house. Instead of answering, the guard demanded to see the tape in the camera. Amin, who always carried two cameras, quickly pushed one under the seat and held out the other with the footage of Bibi. They spent half an hour explaining that they didn't know it was a General's house, and that they were not even filming; Amin showed some footage of Bibi. It was futile. Amin and Kazem were taken to the police station, where they had their possessions taken from them and were locked up in a cell. Their pleas of innocence were ignored. Even the piece of paper that we had obtained earlier from the Ministry of Foreign Affairs, giving us permission to film on the streets, became obsolete. The General himself would have to come in and authorise their release, but he was out at a function that night. They had waited patiently in the small makeshift cell, separated from the young police by rattling metal bars between which, if they wanted to, they could have easily squeezed out. They had been entertained by the guards, teenage boys doing their army service, who spent the evening making prank calls to girls, hanging up on strangers and laughing, or whispering and giggling with their girlfriends over the phone.

The General eventually came, and apologised for the misunderstanding. They were released. But it was a close call. Had the General not been a good-natured man, it could have ended differently.

Another incident occurred on our way back from that trip to Iran when we decided to drive across the border from Herat to Mashhad, instead of flying. My father, who was on assignment in Herat at that time, decided to travel with us.

After a three-hour drive from Herat we reached the border, and thanks to our driver's frequent travels between Iran and Afghanistan, which had made him known to the border guards, we were allowed to drive straight across the no man's land that linked the two countries instead of being made to walk.

Amin, for whom the camera had become a third limb, was filming. As our car was very slowly parting the dense crowd, without any warning, a guard holding a rifle stepped up to us and in one quick and violent motion opened the door to the front seat, grabbed Amin's camera, and slapped him across the face. Instantly, a crowd gathered. Amin did not react and sat in the car, frozen, as our driver and my father ran out. They instructed me to stay in the back seat.

'No filming here!' the guard shouted.

Amin got out, having recovered, somewhat. All he cared about was getting his camera back. 'I am sorry, I didn't know,' he said.

'Give him back his camera,' the driver said, coming to the rescue aggressively.

'No,' the guard shouted. 'He needs to delete the film.'

'I won't do that,' Amin said, raising his voice.

'I won't let you go,' the guard shouted back.

Another armed guard pushed his way in to intervene. The driver started to argue with them. Amin was asking what he could do so they would let us go. My father, keeping calm through this, came around to an observing guard. He tapped him on the shoulder and held out his hand with a fifty-dollar note and said, 'Split it between the two of you and let these kids go.'

The man took the money and spoke to the guard with the camera. 'It's okay. Let him go this time. It's all sorted.'

'What do you mean it's all sorted?' he shouted.

'Don't worry yourself, it's time for your break,' he said. 'Give him back the camera, let's go have some tea. They will take care of him on the other side of the border.'

With that, the other man calmed down and gave Amin back his camera.

We sat in the car, distraught, and drove across in silence, all of us knowing it could have ended badly.

I didn't know whether or not my father had recounted that story to my mother. We never told him or my mother about the food poisoning and night in jail until much later, but he had a lived experience of what Amin and I were going back to. My mother's experience of Afghanistan had been only a week visiting my father at the Intercontinental, though she knew fairly well what we were facing.

I knew what we were facing, too. But I was willing to take the risk.

6

Waiting in the Kabul airport for hours, unable to find Seddiq, the worst possible scenarios were flashing through my mind. I calmed myself and decided that if no one turned up, we would take a taxi to the Intercontinental, have a hot shower and a meal, rest, and get in touch with someone to sort out the situation. As I was mapping out possible escape routes, Amin finally found Seddiq's number. The Iranian-import shopkeeper allowed the use of his mobile phone for overseas calls at exorbitant fees, and Amin had called Soroush, Mahboba's son in Australia, to get Seddiq's number. Mahboba had already left for Kabul. Soroush had to call his aunt in Sydney to get Seddiq's number in Kabul and then Amin had to call him back.

Seddiq had been waiting for us in the car park since we had landed. He had not been permitted entry into the airport. Only special vehicles, convoys and people with tickets could go beyond a certain point. He directed us to walk out of the building towards the car park. Why hadn't anyone, including the guards and the shopkeeper, suggested this to us?

Seddiq was a tall man with a straight back. In the cool March weather he was wearing a long black overcoat, a white shirt, black pants, and a white skullcap over his peppered hair. In his face I could see a resemblance to Mahboba, but his wide nose and broad smile somehow made me think of a lion. It reminded me that he was known as the father of Hope House. He greeted us, apologising for the lack of communication as we crossed the armed barricades that separated the car park from the airport. Beyond this, men squatted next to some barbed wire, awaiting the arrival of their passengers. This may have been a garden some time ago but was now a muddy paddock. Seddiq directed us towards a grey van, where two young men waited. He introduced them as Jameel and Bashir.

Jameel was about twenty-five with dark skin,

curly hair, and wild green eyes. He was wearing a white Afghan *shalwar kameez*, and on top of that a black faux-leather jacket, a common look in Kabul. Bashir, who I saw was twenty when he proudly showed off his university ID, was Jameel's younger brother. He was paler and rounder than Jameel, with kind dark eyes, and short curly hair. Unlike Jameel, he was more Western in his style. His jeans had a metal strap against the front zipper with stars and Xs, which attracted the eye to his crotch. Boss and Diesel labels were lopsidedly stitched to each leg. A crinkly bluish-purple collared shirt topped with a dark jacket turned out to be a combination that he would wear many times during our month-long stay.

The brothers put our bags in the back of the van. In the front window I saw a printed sign: 'Hope House: The Orphanage of Mahboba's Promise'.

We settled into the van, and my concerns were replaced with the excitement of arrival and the awe that the city of Kabul awakens in me every time.

As we drove through the ever-dusty city, I noticed that the streets were cleaner, with less litter and fewer beggars. There were also fewer American soldiers around. On our previous trips we had seen groups of them marching in the street, following a tank. Armed and dressed to fight, with one hand on their rifles, they had walked vigilantly, turning their heads to the right and left in a continuous, synchronised movement. Although they had the power to pull the trigger at any moment, the young men had looked afraid even in all their armour.

This time the Afghan army had replaced them. Soldiers stood confidently tall on the back of green pickups. They patrolled every other street with their weapons resting on stands on the back of the car, ready to shoot. With their heads and faces covered in black shawls, they were much more threatening than the convoys of visibly afraid young American men.

Along the way, Amin and I pointed out familiar buildings like the Iranian embassy, which occupied an entire block; on weekdays hundreds of people would line up here to try their luck at escaping to Iran. The American embassy was also recognisable because it was the most heavily fortified compound in the area, with cement blocks several metres thick. Around the compound, heavily armed guards in helmets and bulletproof vests fearfully eyed every innocent passerby.

Seddiq, Jameel and Bashir joked that we were practically locals. Amin, who likes to blend in quickly in a new environment, responded with an imitated Dari dialect that had everyone laughing.

Along the way I recognised the street where Aryan Bank was located. My father had helped establish it seven years before, and it was still in the same two-storey house with guards permanently planted at its doors. As we drove past, I felt grateful to my father for the opportunity to be in Afghanistan.

After Aryan Bank, we took a wide road and travelled north, and my heart began to pound faster. We had not ventured out of urban Kabul in our previous trips. We crossed different cityscapes: an industrial part with construction materials like metal and wood for sale; an area where alongside the road red, green and bright blue doors stood out against the dusty earth leading nowhere; car yards packed with every make, from Toyotas to Jeeps and even limousines.

Eventually, we reached the foothills where some domestic life appeared again. The air felt fresher here.

Jameel turned the van into a bumpy gravel street. Dividing it were rows of newly planted dust-choked saplings that barely stood up against the weight of the heavy traffic. To our right and left, and all the way to the foot of the mountains, lay empty lots of land, some of which were enclosed by low brick walls and bright doors. Along the way, a few half-finished multi-storey brick houses with large balconies and extravagant statues of lions and eagles decorated the landscape. They were brand new, not bearing any resemblance to the bombed-out mud houses with plastic windows we had seen all around Kabul. We learned that in this area, Kart-e-ye Nejat, the government only allowed the building of brick houses. The high cost of bricks and other building materials meant that many who had land could not afford to build on it, which was why half-built houses dotted the landscape. Still, people lived in these wall-less, damp and dripping structures until they had enough money to finish construction. Some never would.

Finally, we turned left into a bumpier street with a large water-filled ditch at the beginning of it. Jameel carefully manoeuvred around it. From here, the three-storey white and blue building of Hope House became visible. My heart was racing as we approached and Jameel honked the horn. Someone opened the green iron door and we drove under the red and green arch that read 'Mahboba's Promise Hope House'.

Amin held my hand and, squeezing it, said, 'Here we go.'

Part II

7

Our arrival at Hope House, two years after first seeing it on a flyer in Mahboba's office, was unforgettable. As we stepped into the grounds, we were greeted by a line of children with lively and beaming faces. The girls on one side and the boys on the other, giggling quietly, still bundled up in their pink, blue and yellow winter coats, formed a corridor for us to pass through.

In our excitement, we forgot our luggage in the van. When we turned around, a teenage boy was wheeling the bags to a corner. Seddiq signalled him. He came and with a firm handshake welcomed Amin, then put his hand on his chest and bowed his head to greet me. Seddiq introduced him as Abdul Fattah, the groom-to-be and hopefully the star of the film we were making. He broke into a grin, and blushed bright red ear to ear. Amin slapped him on the back, and from that moment Abdul Fattah became our good friend.

Before that day, I had imagined an orphanage would be dull and grim. Hope House was nothing like that. We stepped inside one of the two white and blue buildings; the floor was tiled in emerald green and the walls were painted to match. The storeys above wrapped around and the open space on the ground floor glowed, with sun shining in through a glass roof. Although this was a place where children without parents were taken care of, it felt vibrant, full of positive energy.

We were guided upstairs into a large room with dark pink walls and floral carpets. Its mauve curtains were pulled up in a large knot, revealing an uninterrupted view of the snow-capped mountains that surround Kabul. Children trickled into the room after us. Almost a hundred squeezed in around the walls. Late-comers, teachers and neighbourhood children sat in several rows by the door.

As we sat under the window, the children settled in around us. We curiously observed each other;

Amin and I looked on in silence, smiling, and they looked back with shy giggles and whispered to each other. Were we supposed to say or do something? Several minutes later Seddiq walked in, interrupted the awkwardness and introduced us as their guests from Iran. They were to be polite and treat us like family, he told them. As if on cue, one of the smallest children got up from the end of the room, walked to us, sat on my lap and hugged me. I cuddled him back. Everyone laughed. He had the large eyes and tiny nose of a toddler, but his face was weathered and chapped like an old man's. His tiny hands were rough, tanned and so dry that the skin around his fingers was peeling.

'This is Mojib,' said Seddiq. 'He is three. He is one of the youngest children here without any relatives.'

As I caressed the hair of the tiny boy in my lap, my heart twisted and a lump of sadness grew in my throat. This seed of sorrow would grow into a tree over the next four weeks.

Another awkward silence followed, and the children whispered among themselves. Then I remembered my father had given me a packet of sweets as we were leaving Tehran. I picked up Mojib, who was surprisingly light, and set him on Amin's lap. I got the tin of sweets out of my handbag and went around offering it to the children. Seddiq introduced each of them as I passed.

'Maryam and Arezoo are taekwondo champions.' Two girls sitting hand in hand at the end of the room, one very fair and almost European-looking, and the other of Hazara background, hid their faces with their white scarves and blushed as they took a sweet each.

'We have a lot of taekwondo champions in this room. All the girls are strong and can beat the boys any day.' Everyone chuckled. 'That is Hakim, he is also our taekwondo champion.' A small boy bowed his head.

'Nazanin is one of our teachers here. She teaches kindergarten.' A slim young woman wearing a maroon jacket smiled with crooked teeth. 'Next to her is Rahman, our English teacher.' The young man smiled too, and went bright red.

'Azima is one of our teachers,' Seddiq said of the middle-aged woman with smooth glowing skin. I later learned that her fair appearance hid one of the most difficult lives I would encounter during the entire trip. Azima had nine children, one so severely mentally disabled that he had to be chained to the door to prevent him from escaping.

As we chatted, several of the girls left the room and came back with a ewer of warm water, offering it to us. We washed our hands and dried them with fresh towels as the children watched. Then the older girls and boys left to help with the food. A long piece of thick maroon plastic was rolled along the floor, and as we talked with Seddiq, plates of rice and meat, lots of bread, fruits, salad and bottled water were spread on the floor. The meal was simple and satisfying. The children ate with their hands, slowly and in silence. After they ate, the spread was quickly whisked away by every little hand in the room. The children then disappeared, one by one. Only Mojib still sat on my lap as we spoke with Seddiq while Abdul Fattah and Nazanin brought in flasks of freshly brewed green tea and caramels.

After tea, Abdul Fattah told us he would help us settle into our room. We would not be staying within the walls of the compound, he said, and asked us to grab our things. We left on foot.

8

Hope House was located on a wide street, not yet asphalted, in the foothills of the mountains. It was one of the few properly finished buildings in the area; only a handful of other incomplete structures dotted the landscape in the distance. As it had rained earlier in the day, mud had overtaken the entire street. We walked through it, trotting in the slush, wheeling our equipment behind us, across an empty lot of land to a construction site with a two-storey building.

Abdul Fattah knocked loudly on the rust-coloured door, and a construction worker opened it. We were guided in, past a small skeletal garden. We pulled our luggage up a cement ramp and entered through an unpainted wooden door into a large house where a set of half-built stairs led upstairs.

Workers were heaving loads of materials up and down between the two levels when we entered. The flooring was not yet laid, so we had to skip quickly through the rough cement to a room on the left. This was to be our residence for the next month.

For a moment I was excited about the room. Large windows opened to a humbling vista of the foothills of Kabul. Then as I looked closer, I noticed the dusty carpet that temporarily covered the floor, the plaster on the wall which had not yet been painted and left a white patch on your clothes when you brushed by it. The room contained a large pile of blankets, folded mattresses and some sheets, and nothing else. After we set down our equipment, Abdul Fattah showed us the bathroom across the hallway. It was the only part of this house that was finished. Tiled and shiny, it even had a hot shower, but with limited water pressure. A hot shower with running water, I found out, was a luxury for most people here back then.

Abdul Fattah left us to rest. Before leaving, he told us to lock the door from the inside. It had not occurred to me that we would be in any danger here.

We unrolled the mattresses and the blankets. The

bedding smelled musty but I lay down in it and slept to the sound of hammering and loud instructions yelled between the workers.

About an hour later, we were woken up by Abdul Fattah. 'Amin Agha,' he called repeatedly until Amin opened the door and found him with a large tray of biscuits, sweets and a flask. After a quick cup of green tea, with the sun beginning to set behind the mountains, we dressed to go across to Hope House.

At Hope House, Amin went with Abdul Fattah, and I was taken to Nazanin's kindergarten class. In a room on the second floor all the smallest residents of Hope House were sitting around in a circle on colourful tiles of the English alphabet. When I walked in, Mojib hugged my leg. I picked him up and gave him a gentle whirl. He already felt like family.

Mojib picked up a small toy car, one of the many donations that had travelled around the world before landing here, and started to push it around. The children played and shared toys in small groups. I took pictures of this innocent scene – it could have been any playgroup anywhere in the world, except that here, at the end of the day, there would be no one picking them up, no one helping them wash their faces, brush their teeth and change into their pyjamas. For many, Nazanin was the closest they had to a mother. None of these children had a mother all to themselves, nor a home to return to. Nazanin was extremely careful of the responsibility given to her. She gently caressed each child and kissed them during the session. During the month that we were there, I never saw her shout or become angry, even when the children tested her patience.

Nazanin set a colouring task and with one hour to go, she opened up to me. She was always smiling, but anything that upset her would show in her eyes. As we spoke, I could see the worry and sadness seep through.

Nazanin, about twenty, was one of the oldest girls at Hope House. She used to live in Tehran with her family. She reminisced about the good life they had in Iran, emphasising several times that they had lived 'uptown'. I asked where uptown was. Kan, she told me.

Kan used to be a small village in the north-west

of Tehran. I had very fond memories of it. My family used to go there for picnics in mulberry season. At the end of the day, in one of the many orchards, we would throw a cloth at the foot of a tree and shake the trunk to collect fresh, juicy mulberries. But, over the years, like many areas across Tehran, Kan too had been flattened and turned into apartment blocks. A blue collar outer suburb, it is not considered 'uptown' by any means from a Tehrani perspective. But I also understood why it was for Nazanin, compared to other areas where many Afghans lived and worked.

I hadn't known anything about the way Afghan refugees lived when I was growing up, in the nineteen-eighties. All around our middle-class neighbourhood of Aryashahr, and similar Tehran suburbs of the time, people had begun adding floors to their houses. The neighbour to our left was the first. Soon the family across the street followed, and eventually my father too was lured by the idea of having some extra income by living upstairs and renting out the floor below. As the war between Iran and Iraq seemed to be finishing, those people pouring in from the outer suburbs of Tehran and the villages with the promise of the good city life needed places to stay. And single-storey Tehran wouldn't be able to fit in every hopeful person and family who had been forced to leave their home and farm.

In Tehran's construction boom of the time, most of the work was done by Afghan labourers. They were a significant thread in the fabric of our lives, interwoven with ours and essential, yet at the same time disregarded and despised. As children we avoided them like our life depended on it because of the stories we were told. When my cousin and I were naughty, my aunt threatened that if we didn't behave she would hand us over to the Afghan construction workers across the street. They would cut us open and stuff us with opium and send us across the border as mules. We believed her, and on our way home from school we ran for dear life every time an Afghan worker glanced in our direction. Other children at school had all heard similar stories.

Most Afghan refugees came to Iran after the Soviet invasion of Afghanistan in 1979 and the turmoil that followed, some legally, but most illegally. It is estimated that two million Afghans came after the invasion. While nobody knows this for sure, everyone knows they played a huge part in reconstructing post-war Iran on minimum wages and with no rights. And yet, they were blamed for all sorts of crimes and were depicted as uncultured and backward to the degree that the word 'Afghani' became an insult in Farsi, used to call someone stupid or unrefined.

What we didn't know, in all our stories about them, was how these people who played such a significant part in our lives actually lived. Most Afghan refugees could not legally register their marriages, births or deaths in Iran. Without a legal birth certificate, their children were stateless. Consequently, they could not go to school.

Then, in 2001, when the Taliban was ousted, the Iranian government began to crack down on illegal stays. Hundreds of thousands of Afghans were rounded up and sent back on buses. But this had been a slow process. This was why there had been so many people at the embassy in Tehran, even as late as 2009, when we had gone to apply for our visa. They were there to get passports and register births, deaths and marriages with the Afghan authorities, and to clarify their national status before being deported.

Most had nothing waiting for them on the other side of the border, and would bring with them nothing but their own poverty.

Nazanin and her family had lived in Kan legally for some years. She had loved it there but hated the way they were treated and the conditions of their stay. They had to constantly renew their visas and pay large sums to the government. Even then, they were not allowed to go to public schools, and had very few rights. The situation had become worse. By the end of her family's stay in Iran, any Afghan national was no longer even admitted into public hospitals for treatment.

Nazanin had two sisters and a young brother, Ali, about three, who was in her class. The family had been forced to come back to Afghanistan after their visa was not renewed. Her mother lost her job as a cleaner. Employers who worked by the book did not want to risk hiring illegal workers; the rest, Nazanin said, were sharks who abused the workers and never paid them. They left before the authorities could catch up with them and deport them.

I heard nothing about Nazanin's father, but later

in the trip I met her mother, who lived nearby. She was a modern-looking woman with thickly tattooed eyebrows, a clear sign of Iranian influence. There was a sad look in her eyes though, a distant gaze. Later I heard many at Hope House complain that she spent too much money on herself and not enough on her children, with some claiming that she left her children there while she went to get her hair done and that she bought new clothes every other week. I didn't know her well enough to doubt or believe them. But looking at her wearing make-up, and taking care of herself where other women didn't have the means and education to do so, I understood why they talked about her.

Nazanin herself was a simple girl. She had married one of the boys from Hope House, Rahman, who now taught English to the children. Together, they lived in one of the houses nearby.

After the play session I ventured into the schoolyard, where children clustered in groups. Some were drawing with chalk on the ground, a few were playing hopscotch, while others ran around chasing each other. A few older girls encircled me and asked me to play catch. I was making friends on my first day, recognising some of the girls by name. As they were chasing me, I saw Amin being pulled into a basketball game by the boys. They were playing on the cement court however they could: some barefoot, some with one slipper on and a few in socks.

After a long game of catch I stopped for a break, sat down on the ledge surrounding the garden, and watched the peaceful scene around me. Two girls carried a large tray with a flask of tea and some cups across the yard and into the office. The boys continued to play basketball. A group of younger children emerged from the building, picked up some chalk and began to draw on the ground. Despite the trauma that many of the children had experienced, there was a sense of ease and harmony in this space. After only half a day, I was getting an understanding of the importance of Mahboba's work. I already knew from our previous trips that a lot of children lived perilous lives on the streets of Kabul. Without Mahboba, it would be that many more.

9

When we were in Kabul in March 2006, one of the things that had most struck my heart was the number of orphan children on the streets. In Afghan society the role of the father is so important that when he dies, a child is considered an orphan even if the mother is still alive, because it is only he who can bring income into the family. Thirty years of war and internal conflict have left about two million children orphaned. Sometimes overnight, small boys who were playing games the day before would become the sole breadwinner of their household or left at the mercy of uncles and distant relatives.

On a trip outside Kabul, we stopped in a small settlement for a break. As we walked around, it seemed like most businesses were run by boys, supervised by a few middle-aged or immobile old men. Among them, boys who appeared to be as young as ten or eleven managed and ran grocery shops, worked in dark, dingy tailoring kiosks, baked bread, and carried heavy loads on construction sites. I will never forget the shape of one boy's hands, which had grown much bigger in proportion to the rest of his body. The wheelbarrow he pushed seemed like it had become part of him, as though he had morphed to fit its shape.

While the boys on the outskirts were lucky enough to have access to such jobs in family-run businesses, most in the city didn't have such opportunities. In Koocheh Morgha, I saw how small boys were acting as servants to owners of antique and craft shops, bringing them tea, cleaning and running errands. Those unlucky enough not to have even this kind of job were on the streets selling all sorts of useless items like plastic bags, expired gum and sweets, pens that didn't work, and even matches.

A tiny boy, no more than four, in a stained pink overcoat, with white pants turned grey and a pair of black gumboots ripped at the toes, tugged at my coat. His nose was running and it had dried all across his face, his hair was messy, and his skin looked as rough as a fifty-year-old man's. He was holding on to the box of balloons he was selling as if his life depended on it. He looked up at me with his deep dark eyes. My eyes welled up looking down at him. I put a ten dollar note in his pocket and took one balloon. He took out the money and looked at it, not recognising it. All he knew was that it looked like money. He pushed it deep down into his pocket, smiled at me, and ran away.

I stood frozen until a young girl of maybe ten, dressed in rags, tapped me on the shoulder, trying to sell me gum. I was about to give her some money too, when Kazem, our driver, shouted at her. She jumped up in shock and walked off, holding my gaze. Kazem had to remind me to move along. There were so many of them. A small handout from me was not going to solve anything, he said, and pushed me along.

On the same trip, I made friends with one of the street boys in Koocheh Morgha. Seifi, who was hanging out with a slightly older boy, was about ten, with a fair complexion and crooked teeth. He wore a thick jumper and a pair of pants pulled up to his chest, and carried a small tray of gum. When Seifi and his friend approached us, Kazem almost pushed them aside. I ignored Kazem and talked to Seifi, who tagged along as we walked. He tried to sell me some gum. I told him I didn't want any but gave him some money. He refused. 'I am not a beggar,' he said, almost offended. 'Just take a pack.' I did. He looked at the amount and gave me several packs. As he walked along with us, I asked him why he wasn't at school.

He responded matter-of-factly that his father had died recently, and his older sister was getting married. He needed to use the school holidays to make some money so his mother could sew some new clothes for the wedding.

The next time we went to Koocheh Morgha, I spotted Seifi and his friend again. When they saw us, they ran towards us, as if we were old friends. Both boys had wrapped black rubbish bags around themselves as raincoats, tied around their waists with a string. They tagged along for a while in silence.

Seifi was one of the lucky ones. Years later we recognised him in footage from Uncle Haji's

Orphanage, one of Mahboba's small orphanages in Kabul which had almost closed due to lack of funds. Money was raised thanks to a video report we helped make. Uncle Haji's Orphanage was able to stay open, and even to take on new residents, including Seifi.

A few years later, I learned from a photojournalist I met in Sydney that there were children even more unfortunate than the ones I had seen on the streets. In parts of Afghanistan, young boys are sometimes sold out of desperation and severe poverty. Some are given away to extreme religious groups who brainwash them for suicide bombings; others are sold into a life of sexual slavery. Powerful tribal leaders and warlords buy pre-adolescent boys for entertainment. These boys are made to dress up as women and dance for groups of men. Often, they are repeatedly raped. This practice is called *bache bazi*, which literally means 'boy play'. Because the men who engage in this activity are usually powerful and rich, no one can touch them; any cases that are brought to the media's attention are quickly silenced. In a majority Muslim country where homosexuality is forbidden, such revelations can cause a lot of damage to the reputation of the men involved.

The photojournalist who infiltrated these parties and tried to publicise the resulting photos in Afghanistan was met with death threats and now lives in exile, in Australia. I saw the images for which his life was threatened at the opening of his exhibition. They capture the intimate lives of those who buy and own the boys, and follow some of the children who managed to escape, ending up on the streets, and often addicted to hard drugs.

That was why after my first day at Hope House, I knew the children here, despite everything, were among the lucky ones.

10

On our first night at Hope House we didn't have dinner with the children, who normally ate in one of the large rooms downstairs. We ate in the common room upstairs, lit dimly by a single dangling light bulb. At that time, electricity didn't function properly in the outer suburbs of Kabul, and at night Hope House operated on a weak generator, which gradually faded out altogether. After dinner, as we were having tea and the room grew dimmer and dimmer, most of the children filed in. Seddiq turned on an ancient colour television. He twisted the metal hanger attached to it to receive the fuzzy images. By now some thirty boys and girls huddled together, lost in the fantasy of a badly dubbed Indian soap opera. Mojib sat on my lap, leaning against me comfortably, sucking his thumb. He was floating between reality and dreams.

As the children began to doze off, we decided to retire to our room. Leaving the warmth behind, with Abdul Fattah by our side, we crossed the now eerie plot of land by torchlight, to the sound of the distant howling of dogs. With each step our shoes felt heavier with mud.

In the dark, two stray dogs followed us. My heart began to pound faster and I wanted to run as quickly as I could, but as they kept behind us and wagged their tails, I realised they meant no harm. From then on, they would appear every time we came out of the Hope House doors and escort us across.

Our room, which had been warm during the day, was now a freezer. As we spread out our bedding, still in our parkas, Abdul Fattah ran out. Five minutes later he came back with a heater and a small gas canister. It warmed up immediately with the bright orange glow of the heater's element but the smell of gas filled the room. The hose had a small leak. Abdul Fattah ran back out again and reappeared with some black tape. He tried to fix the hose but we could still smell the gas. He opened the doors and the windows and a cold wind overtook the room again. He couldn't work out exactly where the leak was. So he taped the entire hose, until he could no longer smell it. But I still could. We closed the windows and the door, leaving a tiny gap in the furthest window, hoping we would not die overnight from a slow gas leak.

As we lay down on the musty sheets, the barely glowing light bulb in our room flickered and died out. We were in the dark, with a faint warm glow from the heating element, in a half-constructed house, with Afghan construction workers sleeping in the rooms above. In the uncanny silence of the night, dogs continued to howl in the distance.

As I slowly warmed up under the layers of blankets, I thought about the children at Hope House, eyes heavy with sleep. The smaller children would be sleeping already. The older ones would carry them to their rooms. They would all sleep without a bedtime story, never being properly tucked in, never waking up to a mother's soft voice and kisses in the morning. I fell asleep thinking about the unresolved tension that hung between me and my mother.

11

After I'd walked away from the argument at the dinner table, back in Tehran, Amin had come into our bedroom and said that maybe I shouldn't go with him. I'd turned away, saying there was nothing I could do. My heart broke for my mother.

The next day, a cousin called me.

'Feel for your mother,' she told me. 'Do you know how much I wish my own mother was still with me and would worry about my safety? Don't fight her so much.'

Later that day, I had a serious conversation with my mother where I listened again to her concerns and explained my decision to go. We fell asleep in each other's embrace. For the first time in nights, she slept until sunrise, but I knew she still didn't believe me when I said there was nothing to worry about.

This tug and pull continued the three months we were in Iran, and left me in great conflict. I felt drained.

And then, with a few weeks to go before we were due in Kabul, the man who was to be the producer for the film had not raised a cent. As a result, we had no money, not even to buy our plane tickets. Amin confronted him through email. It didn't go well. We were so thrown by his response that Amin decided to cancel our trip. He emailed our apology to everyone, declaring that we were unable to go. My mother was happy. We were shattered.

That night, I didn't sleep. Had we made the right choice? The change in circumstance had lifted a huge weight from my mother's chest, and transferred it to mine. Could I live with this? Pulling out of the project now would mean the end of our friendship with Mahboba. It would be the end of the rope for something we had started three years before and worked hard to achieve. It would mean that the story of the marriage and the importance of Mahboba's work would remain untold. I tossed and turned all night. I whispered my concerns into Amin's ear sometime in the darkest hours, somewhere between here and the dream world.

In the morning I found Amin in my arms weeping in his sleep. He woke up frowning. Had we made the right decision? He spent several hours with his head under the pillow and didn't get up until midday, and I stayed next to him.

Two days passed mostly in bed. Should we plan to go back to Sydney now? Should we email everyone again and say that's what we would do, and overlook the failure?

On the third day we were still in bed, depressed and confused, when Mahboba called. She had just heard about the situation. She had spoken to the supposed producer, and he was to apologise. She was sorry for the way it had turned out but needed us to make the film for the children's sake. All three of us saw that beyond the marriage we were to follow, the film was needed to promote the work of Mahboba's Promise. If we did this, she reminded us, great things would come out of it, not only for us, but also for the children. 'If money is an issue,' she said, 'Mahboba's

Promise will cover your tickets, and you can return it to us gradually.'

We knew what we should do.

It was then early March. We were to be in Kabul with Mahboba near the end of the month. We left the bed and dressed as soon as Mahboba hung up. Nou Rouz was coming up, and Amin had become involved in another film idea in Iran. This was to take him away from Tehran for several days. He would have to come back from that trip, pack, and be ready to leave for Kabul almost immediately.

My father and I drove to the Afghan embassy several times, slowly and painstakingly, through the jam-packed New Year streets of Tehran. We waited, pushed, argued with bureaucrats. In the end I submitted every senseless thing I was asked for, maybe in time, or maybe not.

The holidays kicked in. I called our travel agent on his mobile phone and told him there was a chance we would need to change our tickets because we may not get our visas in time. He told me to wait until the last day.

I could see the relief in my mother's face.

Then a surprise call came at midday on a public holiday, two days before our departure. My father went to the closed embassy to pick up the passports from a mysterious person behind a small window, where we had been handed our application forms.

As soon as the visas came, I started to pack our equipment and clothes. By the time Amin came back from his trip, I was ready to go. Exhausted after filming for over twelve hours on a bus journey from the south of Iran, he had to unpack his bags, clean his filming gear and reset himself, ready to leave the next day on another huge adventure.

I didn't see my mother that day. She stayed in bed.

12

We were woken up by Abdul Fattah's loud knocks at about seven in the morning, well after the construction workers had already started hammering, calling out to each other, and carrying things up and down the stairs. We had survived the leaking gas. Accompanied by the dogs who emerged as soon as we stepped out, we followed Abdul Fattah to Hope House, where we were greeted with a simple breakfast of flat bread and cheese.

Mahboba was to arrive at around midday and the children were getting ready and making sure everything was immaculate. It had been several years since Mother Mahboba had come to Afghanistan. Girls and boys were washing the floors and cleaning their rooms. Some of the older girls were dabbing on a slight touch of make-up in their rooms. Two small girls were hand-washing clothes on the muddy floor at the back of the toilet blocks. One was wetting the garments in icy water while the other lathered them in detergent in a bucket of hot water that she kept topping up from a huge boiling kettle. Then they would rinse them out, wringing the clothes together as hard as they could with their tiny hands, before hanging them to dry. Their hands were raw by the end of the process.

It was heart-breaking watching the girls do this. Later I narrated this to some of my friends in Hong Kong who had small children. They decided that instead of gifts for their wedding anniversary, they would ask their friends to donate money towards buying a washing machine for Hope House. A few months later we heard that a washing machine had appeared thanks to their donation.

The preparations were still going when we got into the van with Seddiq, Bashir and Jamil, and headed to the airport.

We were ready to start making a film, but we still had no idea about the direction that things would take. The camera had become part of Amin's body as he set out to capture every moment. While Amin put his effort into recording images, I began to write the stories that were not recorded on film, the intimate human moments and connection, the moments of joy, fear, terror, happiness and love that we experienced in the process of shooting the footage, the surprise of encounters with strangers who would become almost as close as family. With Mahboba in Kabul deep connections would begin to grow between all of us. These things, not captured on film, were part of the story too, and they would stay with us long after we left Kabul.

It all began to unfold and take shape with Mahboba's arrival. She walked out of the airport with a slim Australian woman wearing a green scarf around her hair, a black coat reaching above her knees, and a short jacket that matched her scarf. Walking along with them was also Siar, the boy Mahboba had nursed for an entire year in Australia, after a complicated operation. We had met him in Sydney when he was bent double by his illness; I was elated to see him upright.

After hellos and welcomes, and after Siar was safely handed back to his family, we walked past the barricades and boarded the van, where Mahboba finally introduced us to Virginia Haussegger.

Virginia was an Australian journalist who wrote on women's issues, and was often invited to host events for various organisations. It was at one of these gatherings that she had met Mahboba. After the function, Mahboba had invited Virginia to come to Afghanistan to see the situation for herself. The invitation had been very casual. Mahboba invites everyone she meets to come to Afghanistan; few seriously consider taking up the offer. Virginia did. Several months later, when Mahboba was getting ready for her trip, she was surprised to hear that Virginia had accepted and made plans to come. She had joined Mahboba in transit in Dubai, where they had boarded the plane to Kabul.

Virginia is a seasoned journalist who has previously reported from war zones like Iraq. In the van, despite the chaos outside of the car as we drove across Kabul, she appeared calm and composed. She called her husband to tell him she had arrived safely.

Mahboba's arrival at Hope House was a celebration. A welcome banner ushered her onto the grounds. Fifty or so girls lined up to hand her plastic flowers. She kissed every single one and took her time talking to them intimately. Virginia shook the hands of all the other girls and boys. The children retained the queue until Mahboba reached the end. Only then did the young boys rush towards her and some much-awaited confetti was thrown over her head. The smallest children latched on to her arms and legs, kissing her hands and face. Mahboba gave the older boys a peck on the forehead and they kissed her on the hand in return.

Mahboba was dragged into the common room upstairs by the youngest children. We followed, camera at hand. Others lagged behind us. Just as they had done at our arrival, everyone crammed into the room, but this time there was no awkward shyness. Their mother was visiting them. They piled on top of each other and climbed as close as they could to Mahboba. Virginia sat next to her with a huge smile. Some of the women brought in round frame drums, celebrating the moment with simple repetitive beats.

The children started dancing. The younger girls

moved to some practised choreography and the boys freely jumped up and down. Someone pulled Virginia up. She shook her body, a cause for much amusement for the children. Virginia copied what the girls did and a little dance-off made everyone laugh. They wanted to know what to call her. When she said 'Virginia,' they repeated, 'Giginia,' followed by giggles. Giginia's nickname would stick with her until she left Kabul.

The dancing continued in one corner. In the other, smaller boys and girls were clinging to Mahboba. Some were massaging her back, others caressing her hands and arms. Mahboba kissed their faces, foreheads and hands as they came to her, making sure she held each of them for a while. After all, she was the only mother many of them knew, and they only saw her a few weeks every few years, if they were lucky. Even then, this was probably as much time as they would get to spend physically close to her. We knew her visits were always filled with work on her projects. On this month-long trip she had several matters to attend to, one of the biggest being Abdul Fattah and Fatemeh's wedding.

13

After the children had filled themselves up with Mahboba's love, we had a meeting in the office and Seddiq gave us the backstory over cups of green tea.

Fatemeh, whom we hadn't met yet, was a fifteen-year-old who lived with her father and three siblings across the valley from Hope House. She had lost her mother during the Taliban while her father was in prison for reasons we never discovered. Fatemeh was forced to take care of her two young brothers while her older brother provided for them. When they were brought to Mahboba's attention, Mahboba's Promise helped them. Fatemeh regularly attended school and classes at Hope House. When her father was eventually freed, the children were released into his care. As they were without any source of income, Mahboba's Promise had set them up in the house across the valley, where they still lived.

But Nik Mohammad, Fatemeh's father, had not come back to his family a well man. More than anything else he was affected by the shock of his young wife's unexpected death. He believed that she had not been killed but instead taken and somehow used in the war in Afghanistan by the Bush administration. A while after his return, he decided that his teenage daughter must be married as soon as possible. He was so desperate to marry Fatemeh off that for a few days he sat next to his house and offered her to anyone passing by who might be willing to take her hand. Luckily, they lived in a place where not many people happened to pass by.

When news of this reached Hope House, Seddiq became enraged. He tried to reason with him. But Nik Mohammad was persistent. Nobody at Hope House could change his mind; in the end, they contacted Mahboba in Australia for advice.

To save Fatemeh from a marriage to an old man, Mahboba had suggested that Abdul Fattah consider marrying Fatemeh instead. Initially the shy seventeen-year-old, who taught at Hope House and was a mentor for many of the children, said that he found it inappropriate. But eventually he had begun to notice Fatemeh and fell in love with the quiet girl. Nik Mohammad had agreed to their marriage, and they had got engaged in a small ceremony. After a while, though, Nik Mohammad demanded a dowry beyond anyone's means before he'd let the marriage take place.

This is how the story had reached the impasse it was in now.

One of Mahboba's missions on this trip was to see this union through. Everyone knew the consequences of a bad marriage in Afghanistan. I had seen the horrendous effects first-hand. As we sat in the office and heard the story in detail, I ached with the thought of what might become of Fatemeh if the wedding didn't happen.

14

In 2006, while in Herat, and making *Hidden Generation*, Amin, camera in hand, and I had wandered through the ancient centre of the city on a Friday when it was quiet, exploring the timeless bazaar. We had followed the labyrinth of empty lanes, turning right and left instinctively, without a destination; we eventually came out of the bazaar and crossed a main street, passed a small bakery and turned into a narrow unpaved lane. Lined with a tall straw wall on one side and a row of two-storey mud houses on the other, this narrow passage was extremely bright. The midday sun was shining directly from above, and a lone shadowless burqa-clad woman walked into the dark mouth of a tunnel at the end of the lane. We walked behind her in silence.

At the end of the cool tunnel, a bright light was shining through a small open door. Without a second thought we walked in. We found ourselves in the courtyard of an ancient two-storey building. It was only then we realised we had wandered into someone's house. We were turning back when an elderly man who was mending some broken plant pots on the other side of the garden said a loud hello. He left his tools and headed over to greet us. I felt uneasy: we were intruders. Amin said hello, apologised, and explained that we were filmmakers and had lost our way. We were leaving. The man wiped his hands on a small cloth and instead invited us in for tea.

The building that wrapped around the courtyard was not an ordinary residence. It was made of ornate small bricks that formed a distinct pattern across the wall. Further in, several wide steps led up to a huge wooden door. The top floor had massive windows with intricate geometric shapes. In the old days, this must have been either a school, a university or a palace.

As we marvelled at the architecture, the elderly

man led us to the far side of the courtyard and through a wooden door to his quarters. It was freshly painted aqua green and intricate engravings carved into the wall, shaped like narrow waisted vases, were coloured bright pink. The floor was covered with old floral carpets. In the afternoon light that came through the window dressed with thin lace, ancient dust particles were dancing in mid-air.

Several cats made their way into the room, meowing, as we settled ourselves on the floor across from the man and a small boy who brought us a kettle of tea. The room was cool despite the heat outside. From where I was sitting I could feel a cold draft from a door half-open to a dark room behind me. I peered in. I could make out the shapes of construction tools, a wheelbarrow and shovels, stacked inside.

Leaning against the large pillows next to the window, the elderly man welcomed us. He lived here with his son, who had recently been released from prison. They lived on the other side of the courtyard, on the upper level of the main building. He was interested in what we were doing.

Amin explained that we were making a film, investigating the reasons why so many women in

Herat burnt themselves. Did he have an opinion on this topic?

Of course he did. As Amin set up the camera and wired him up with a microphone, the man cleared his throat and began.

'In the name of God the compassionate the merciful,' he started in Arabic, and continued as if conducting a lecture, 'suicide is a sin in Islam. One of the biggest anyone can commit. What makes anyone commit a sin?'

Silence from us.

'Ehhh…it is very simple, you know this. Satan. Satan, and nothing else! Satan tempts these women, they go crazy, and then they burn in hell.' He said those words with such vehemence pointing his finger at some invisible force in front of him that it made me shiver.

'If you look at the history of our religion, it has always been said that women should follow men. Why? Because women can't think for themselves. They are stupid. When women want to think for themselves, then Satan can easily come into their hearts and the hearts of their family.'

He paused for dramatic effect.

I cringed. I wanted to run out.

He continued, 'Satan is very powerful. He can trick anyone into thinking that life can be better. Women, who don't know any better, who are stupid, believe him. When they want things their husband can't buy, when they want to think on their own, Satan creeps in. He whispers into their ears at night when they can't sleep. There is no way out but to kill themselves. To commit a sin, so they will not go to heaven. Satan wins.'

I knew this kind of opinion still existed all across Afghanistan among the older generation. These were men who believed that women were to do nothing but what God, the prophet and their husbands instructed them to do. Neither Amin nor I saw any point in challenging this ancient opinion. Instead we listened as he finished his monologue. He spoke for about half an hour, repeating the same point from different angles, with various examples. When there was a slight pause, Amin quickly but politely signalled 'enough' with his hands. The man stopped. There was a stretch of silence, a self-congratulating pause on this thought-out opinion piece.

I breathed. It was over.

Then he volunteered to show us the rest of the citadel. I later found out that the building had been one of four synagogues in Herat before the Taliban. It was used as housing while in the process of being restored and eventually transformed into a school. We followed the old man across the courtyard, camera and boom in hand. We went up the few grand steps into the main part of the building. He knocked on the large ornate door, and seconds later his son, daughter-in-law and several small children appeared. His son, who introduced himself as Ali, had a moustache and tattoos all over his hands in a design that ran up under his long-sleeve shirt. He invited us in as his wife and children disappeared.

This part of the house had exceptionally high ceilings with fresh white and blue paint and colourful floral plaster decorations. The floor was covered with several red and green carpets. Ali lit a small gas cylinder in the makeshift kitchen next to the window and boiled some water for tea. We sat on the floor and leaned against the large red cushions. A small television sitting on a few bricks was showing a Bollywood music video on mute.

As he squatted by the window, waiting for the

water to boil, Ali casually informed us that he had been released from prison only a few days before. He was very happy to be back with his family. He was innocent but his father didn't believe him, no one ever did. Yes, he did smoke opium, but that did not make him a dealer or a liar. 'But no one ever believes me.'

Amin asked for permission to film. Ali granted it and asked what the film was about. As Amin explained, Ali picked up a small glass, put some hot water in it and rolled the water from glass to glass to clean them for tea. They still looked grimy, in need of a good scrub. He poured tea into the glasses as Amin asked his opinion on the reasons women across Afghanistan were burning themselves.

He thought for a moment and then spoke about violence against women.

'There are lots of hurtful acts towards women in this country,' he said. 'In this area, several months before I was jailed, a man had suspected his wife of being unfaithful. She had gone to the markets. He staked out by the bakery and waited until her return. Then suddenly he pounced on her and slit her stomach with a hunting knife right on the street in front everyone. All her insides fell out onto the ground. You would have passed the place when you entered the alley.' He paused. I did remember the bakery.

Amin asked him if he had heard of women who burn themselves. Not many, he replied, but there had been a case in this neighbourhood about a year before. A newly married young woman was very unhappy about her life. She had told everyone she was going to kill herself. No one had believed her.

'One night,' he told us animatedly, 'she crawls out of bed and slips into the basement. She ties her own feet to a pole so that she can't move or free herself, to make sure she does not survive. She pours petrol all over herself and lights a match. The family wake up for prayer at dawn with the stench of the young bride's charred body. I can show you the place where it happened.'

I shivered at his words.

'Really?' Amin said. 'Is it far?'

'No, no, not at all, it is just on the way to here. You must have passed it.'

We packed our equipment, retracing our steps into the dark tunnel we had come through. We stopped at one of the green doors. It was tightly shut. He knocked loudly several times but no one responded. 'Friday,' he said, 'people go out, people go to prayers.'

The door next to it, though, was ajar. It was the same one that we had walked past on our way in, noticing it because it had moved, kept opening and closing slightly as if by itself, though there was no breeze.

'I can show you the house through here.'

Another shiver ran down my spine. Of all the streets, of all the houses, of all the places, why had we been guided to this particular one?

Ali knocked on the open door. A small girl peered out and he asked her to call her parents. She ran in and came back with a young woman wearing a pink scarf and holding a baby. The girl looked more like an older sister than a mother. He told her that we were making a film and wanted to peer out through their balcony to the house next door where the girl had killed herself.

'Not a very good thing to remember, poor thing,' she said, 'but come in.'

She took us up a series of mud steps into her house where a balcony overlooked another yard. She pointed down. 'That is where it happened.'

The garden below was barren, abandoned and dusty. Right at the end of it was the basement. Its windows had been replaced by thick plastic and its wooden door was locked with a large padlock.

'That is where the woman scorched to death,' Ali said dramatically.

The young mother standing next to me clicked her tongue in disbelief. 'It was horrible. I remember. God forbid.'

She paused, then almost whispered, only in my ear, 'The world must know what happens to Afghan women.'

All the hair on my arms stood up and I felt a cold chill through my body. My hands began to shake.

Before we bid Ali farewell, Amin asked him one more question. 'Why do you think these women kill themselves?'

Unlike his father, he responded with facts. 'The girls and women who come back from Iran – and there are many of them in Herat – bring with them a different culture. They are more educated and freer than those who grew up here. The women who have always lived in Afghanistan see their liberation, their education, and feel sad about their own lives here. They have no choice so they kill themselves.'

His response was in line with others we had heard throughout Herat and Kabul.

After the Taliban was ousted and Iran had begun rounding up illegal Afghan refugees and deporting them, thousands upon thousands of people crossed the border once again. We saw hundreds on our way out of Herat a few days later, tired-looking men and women with crying children, pushing carts piled high with suitcases, bags and boxes. Those who could not afford to hire a cart were balancing bundles on their heads and dragging heavy suitcases behind them. They didn't rush and clamber over a fence as they had in my dream. They walked the barren landscape slowly, as if they hoped that somewhere in the no man's land between this border and the next the laws would change and they could just walk back to Iran.

For many the trip in this direction was a return to a barely recognisable homeland, now destroyed and desolate. Both for those who remembered and for those who didn't, this was a trip of lost opportunities. Seeing some of the returning young women, dressed in less modest Iranian clothing and not the burqa, I could anticipate the troubles they would face.

According to the doctors and nurses we talked to, many women who returned became depressed in the face of poverty, homelessness, culture shock, and the loss of freedoms. The added pressure, then, of tribal and family traditions, say in a difficult marriage, could be enough to push them to suicide.

15

At the heart of it, what was really preventing Nik Mohammad from allowing Fatemeh to marry Abdul Fattah was that Abdul Fattah was a penniless orphan. In Afghanistan, the dowry amount is negotiable. But Abdul Fattah had nothing to negotiate with. Aside from a very poor and elderly mother somewhere in the province of Takhar, he had nothing and no one in the world to support him except Mahboba. Abdul Fattah was one of the first children saved by Mahboba's initiative.

I was told that when Abdul Fattah was four, his father died in an earthquake. His mother was left with nothing to support her children. When she heard of some family friends going to Pakistan in search of a better life, she sent her very small son with them. But the better life ended in a refugee camp at the border of Pakistan where Abdul Fattah was left to fend for himself. Apparently there were many children like him. A group of them found each other scavenging for food and shelter and bonded over survival. They went from tent to tent begging for food nobody had to spare. He lived like this for three years until Mahboba took him in.

In 1992 Mahboba was living in Australia. She had recently lost her six-year-old son, Arash, in a drowning accident in Kiama, in New South Wales. Depressed and hopeless, she forced herself to run English and swimming classes for other Afghan women. It was during this time that she had received a letter from her friend Dr Nasrine, a young woman who volunteered in Pakistani refugee camps. Dr Nasrine wrote about the abhorrent conditions for women and children in the camps. In particular, she was concerned about a group of boys who could die in the cold because they didn't have any shelter or food. Moved by the letter, Mahboba mobilised the women in her class and collected one hundred and twenty dollars for Dr Nasrine.

Some months later, a return letter bearing the thumb prints of the children told Mahboba that the money had bought tents and saved their lives. Once Mahboba realised the impact of her actions, the foundations of Mahboba's Promise were formed. She continued to support the children through Dr Nasrine. Abdul Fattah was one of the boys who continued to receive Mahboba's care in Pakistan. The others disappeared. Gradually he became close to Mahboba and her cause, helping her find and save other children at the camp. He eventually moved back to Afghanistan with Mahboba's support and at a young age became a responsible team member of the growing organisation by taking care of younger children.

Now at seventeen he was one of the leading carers. Over the years, he had taught himself to speak decent English, picked up some French from visitors, and learned Arabic. He had memorised the whole of the Qur'an and for this he was nicknamed Qari, one who can recite the Qur'an by heart. In addition to being an all-round mentor, he taught various simple classes to the children. But now, after all those years, with Mahboba as his only support, he couldn't move on to the next stage of his life.

Mahboba told us that she would have helped him through Mahboba's Promise, but the amount that Nik Mohammad wanted for Fatemeh's hand in marriage was beyond her means. Almost ten thousand US dollars was a lot of money by any standard. This money, Nik Mohammad had said, he wanted to save for the marriage of his oldest son. When his son was to marry someone, he too would have to pay a reasonable amount to his future bride's family.

Beside the dowry, there was another reason for Nik Mohammad's reluctance to let his daughter marry Abdul Fattah. Fatemeh was the only female member of his small family. With two young sons, he worried that if Fatemeh left, there would be no one to cook, clean, and care for the children.

Seddiq had offered a solution. He knew that Nik Mohammad wanted a wife for his eldest son as soon as possible, to do the domestic work in place of Fatemeh. He was asking for the money to find a wife for his son anyway. Instead of giving him the money directly, Seddiq suggested he and Mahboba find a wife for his son. Nik Mohammad had agreed.

With this agreement, Seddiq sent out an army of women to find a suitable wife for Nik Mohammad's son. But several months of searching among women near and far had been fruitless.

Nik Mohammad's son, whom we had not met and whose name we were never to learn, was not a particularly eligible bachelor, not very educated, and still doing some kind of military training. People didn't want to marry off their daughters to boys without a secure job.

That Nik Mohammad's family was of the minority Uzbak background also made it more difficult to find a suitable match. Afghan people usually like to marry within the same ethnic group to ensure cultural understanding and continuity.

Added to this, any potential candidates who had overlooked these issues still wanted some money for the hand of their daughter in marriage. Just as Abdul Fattah had to pay Nik Mohmmad, he, too, would have to pay his future daughter-in-law's family. And he didn't have any money. If anyone was to end up paying, it would be Mahboba's Promise. Mahboba said there were no funds for this.

When we entered into the story to make the film, the couple had been engaged for some months. A traditional man, Nik Mohammad was beginning to feel antsy. He said to Seddiq that he was losing face among his neighbours and friends. His daughter was engaged but not yet married, which in the Afghan tradition was very shameful. He now controlled Fatemeh's every move. He prevented her from going to school or contacting Abdul Fattah. Abdul Fattah had saved some money and bought Fatemeh a mobile phone, and sneaked it to her through some of the girls. But Nik Mohammad found out about it and confiscated it.

For months, the only way Abdul Fattah and Fatemeh could find out how the other was doing was through the girls who were allowed to visit Fatemeh. They reported that when she was trapped in the house, she would sit behind the barred window of their sparsely furnished room. For days on end she watched everyone's movement at Hope House across the small valley, waiting to glimpse Abdul Fattah. She wrote letters to him and smuggled them out through her friends. In the letters she commented on things like what Abdul Fattah wore, asking him why he was late to class, even told him he looked nicer without glasses.

By the time Mahboba arrived to try and set the marriage in motion, no one had seen Fatemeh in weeks. Mahboba was determined to get the young couple settled before she returned to Australia, yet the process was proving to be much harder than anticipated.

We began to feel the pressure on the making of this film from the day Mahboba arrived. In finding the topic, we had gone through many phases, promises, obstacles and near-misses; the process had affected every aspect of our lives. We could not afford to fail now.

16

A while after we had first met Mahboba in 2007, the ABC broadcast a *Four Corners* report called 'Afghanistan Unveiled'. It followed a reporter who travelled through Afghanistan investigating issues affecting women. After visiting orphanages and addressing young girls' education, she ended up at the burns unit of the hospital in Herat, where she briefly introduced self-immolation. This, she said, was a new problem in Afghan society, particularly in Herat. Although the program did touch upon the issue, it failed to examine in depth the reasons behind the increase of self-immolation in Herat.

Amin and I had visited the hospital featured in the *Four Corners* report, and were very familiar with the specific reasons why women burn themselves and the impact on their lives. We had seen the horrid condition of women in the burns unit of that hospital. And yet this was not the reality that the *Four Corners* episode showed, and it left me furious.

Soon after the program had screened, I went to see Mahboba. She was upset too. 'They always go to these Muslim countries,' she complained, 'and report back horrible stories without follow up. I want to know what happened to the women that they showed who had burned themselves. What's the point of showing this if no one follows it up?'

Mahboba finally understood the importance of making a film about this issue. But we still had no identifiable character that we could follow to sustain a feature film.

Several months passed without any progress. One afternoon I came across a new page on the Mahboba's Promise website: 'The Burning Women of Kabul Appeal'. It featured a young woman, Lina, with a black scarf covering her entire face, except for her eyes. She was pointing her bare arms towards the camera, showing extensive burn scars.

'The Burning Women of Kabul'. Had we found

the title and subject of our film? I gave Mahboba a call.

Soon after hearing about women's self-immolation from us, and seeing 'Afghanistan Unveiled,' Mahboba was convinced that there was an epidemic. She was particularly concerned about the women who survived and had nowhere to go after their recovery. She had called *Four Corners* and asked them what were they doing about the women they had interviewed. They had responded with something vague that infuriated her. When her friend Kabir, an Australian artist and photographer, was heading to Afghanistan, Mahboba asked him to investigate the issue. She had him go to the 110 Bed Hospital in Herat and report on what he saw. Several days after his departure, Kabir had called Mahboba and told her about Lina, a young woman he had met at the hospital. She had burned herself and survived but had nowhere to go after her release.

The story, as they were told, was that Lina was born in Iran to illegal refugee parents. In December 2003, when she was sixteen, she lost both her parents in the earthquake that hit the historic Iranian city of

Bam. Lina and her brother survived, but he soon disappeared. Lina was abandoned, with only a distant uncle somewhere in Bam. When her uncle heard about Lina's survival, he came and found her at a friend's house. With no source of income, she and her uncle had nowhere to go. In the winter cold, they roamed the streets during the day and slept under bridges at night. Eventually the police, who by now were on the look-out for illegal Afghan refugees, caught up with them. They had no proper documents, and along with hundreds of others, they were rounded up and deported back to Afghanistan.

Over the border, with no money and no contacts, they found themselves stranded. Her uncle, fearing for Lina's safety, quickly made some friends and arranged for her marriage to someone she had not met and whom he didn't know all that well himself. She suddenly found herself in a family with an entirely different culture and with expectations she could not fathom. Growing up in Iran she had been brought up differently to her very conservative in-laws who had never left Afghanistan.

Somehow – just how was never clarified to Kabir – she was either divorced, let go, or ran away, and with nowhere to go and no one to turn to roamed the streets for a few days. She had enough money to eat but not enough for a decent place to sleep. She slept wherever she could on the streets until the police picked her up. But instead of helping her, they jailed her. She was in prison for a few days when one of the officers decided she was a potential wife for his son. With her agreement – although she had not met him – he arranged for their marriage. After several months, for reasons Lina never disclosed, this marriage, too, failed.

Lina was once again left alone, back on the streets. This time she was forced into prostitution. The police caught her again and put her in a different jail. It was this time that she burned herself with the gas cooker they were given to make tea and basic food. As she set herself alight, she really had hoped to die. But prison staff and the other inmates had put out the small fire. The prison released her into the hospital's care. With no real charges pending, after she had recovered from burns on her arms, she was free to go. But she had nowhere to go from there.

It was then, just as she was about to be discharged, that Kabir found her and mentioned her to Mahboba.

She organised for Lina to be taken to Kabul, where she could stay temporarily at Hope House. After a few weeks there, she fell in love with a young doctor who checked on the residents. When I spoke to Mahboba, there was talk of arranging their marriage.

The wedding would make a great story for a film. We wanted to follow Lina in her recovery and see her through the successful marriage. Her story would be the link that would tie together the situation of Afghan refugees in Iran, their desperate return, women's self-burning, prostitution, poverty and Mahboba's efforts in helping these women. The marriage and the love story would give the film the happy twist we wanted. It was all perfect. We set this idea into motion.

Several weeks passed. Amin and I redrafted all our proposals, making Lina the central character. We began to talk to new producers, who showed great interest. When we wanted to get Mahboba's consent on something, I called her. When I asked her about the date of the wedding, there was a slight hesitation in her tone. She told me that Lina was perhaps not the best subject for a film. She had too many problems and a dark side. She had set fire to rooms in the Hope House three times. One of the rooms had been badly burned before the other girls put out the fire. She also caused other problems: she wanted men, Mahboba said. She had tried to sneak men into the orphanage and Mahboba was finding her a big threat to the safety and moral education of the children. She wanted to remove her from Hope House as soon as possible and so did not want Lina to be the subject of the film.

After a few moments of shock I asked her if we could work around this. Mahboba admitted that she had actually already found somewhere safe and sent her away. She just hadn't known how to break the news to me.

With Lina gone, we deleted all the proposals we had spent many weeks writing. Without this story, we also had no film.

After that blow, our interest in the possibility of making a film had waned, and the circumstances of our lives also took us away from the project. Amin was offered work in Melbourne, and I was invited to teach creative writing in Hong Kong. Amidst a house move, a month in Melbourne and a few in

Hong Kong, our plan to make a film in Afghanistan was becoming unattainable, almost forgotten.

It was not until late 2008, during a phone conversation while we were in Hong Kong, that Mahboba mentioned the potential wedding between Abdul Fattah and Fatemeh. It had been this vague and undirected idea that revived our interest again and for which we risked everything and returned to Kabul.

17

Even though we felt no closer to the marriage we had come to film, Mahboba's arrival in Kabul gave us a sense of security. But that afternoon, Mahboba packed Virginia in the van and went to stay at a cousin's house. Amin and I felt awkward, somewhat neglected. We spent the afternoon at Hope House, playing with the children. Once again, they ended the day stacked in front of the television, and we retired to our freezing room escorted by dogs.

The reason for Mahboba's move became clearer early the next day, when she and Virginia returned to Hope House. We followed them to the office and crammed onto the springless brown sofas. As Seddiq went about his business and Mahboba got caught up with some of the young girls, Virginia checked her email. Suddenly her expression changed and she voiced her concern out loud. She had received an email from the Australian Department of Foreign Affairs and Trade, warning that the lives of foreign journalists in Afghanistan were in danger.

Virginia had reported from much riskier places, including Iraq. But on those assignments she had been protected by armed guards and bulletproof cars. She had not expected her bodyguards here to be Mahboba's young cousins, Jameel and Bashir, and her mode of transport a dilapidated van with a cracked windshield.

Virginia asked whether perhaps she should at least register herself with the Afghan Department of Foreign Affairs, as we had done on our previous trip. Mahboba assured her that remaining low-key and private would be in her best interest: anyone could have access to the list of foreign journalists, and by registering she could put herself on a hit list. Mahboba had also discouraged us from registering and we had taken her advice. But a tinge of worry remained in Virginia's expression for the rest of the day, and she wandered about cautiously.

That night Mahboba asked us to take our gear and move to her cousin's house with her and Virginia. We gladly packed our bags from the freezing room and followed.

Mahboba's cousin lived on a wide street lined with two-storey houses in a suburb about half an hour's drive from Hope House. We arrived in the dark. Although there were lampposts, they were inoperative. As we stepped out of the van, our feet sank ankle-deep in mud. Skipping across, Mahboba knocked loudly. A young boy opened the door. After greetings and kisses, the entire family, including several young girls and children, came to the door. As soon as he came out, the husband started to complain that despite the generator the light on the outside had been turned off because of some loose wiring. To Virginia's surprise, he took some wires that were hanging above the door, unwrapped some electric tape and began to strike them together to create a connection. The two live wires sparked.

Virginia winced and let out an odd giggle. 'That's really dangerous. I haven't seen anything like this since I was a very little girl.'

Mahboba translated this and the family laughed.

The lamp above the door lit up and we cheered. The boys took in our luggage and we followed. We took off our shoes, stepping onto a thick plastic that they had laid on the carpet to avoid getting mud into the house.

We were guided into a room that, like most rooms in Afghan houses, had a sheet hanging in the doorway for privacy. Large lilac-coloured cushions were lined up along the walls. The windows were dressed with thick white sheets covered by glittery lilac lace. It was the warmest room I had been in since our arrival. We sat down, and Mahboba's cousins brought us some green tea. The family lounged on the cushions. Drinking the earthy hot green tea, I felt my body warm up.

As Mahboba's family sat around talking, occasionally translating a topic of conversation to English, Virginia remained observant, quiet. Even when we made an effort to include her, she did not engage. When a dinner of meat, rice and vegetables was served, she didn't touch her plate. She excused herself and went to bed. After she left, Mahboba told us Virginia had been disturbed by the emails she had received that morning. But we didn't know the full extent of her worries.

Soon we were taken upstairs where there were three rooms. One where the cousin's son and his wife and children slept, a guest room, where Amin and I were staying, and a smaller room with a rare bed where Virginia was housed. Jameel and Bashir were to sleep in the hallway behind our doors. Our room was a replica of the one below except with a gold colour scheme. We were given blankets and crisp sheets.

We even had access to a very clean bathroom with a proper toilet and a sink inside the house. As there was no running water in the house we had to draw water with a small bowl from two buckets to wash our faces. This was also how we were to shower. We were told, however, to strictly avoid 'going heavy' in this toilet as the plumbing had problems, so for number two, Mahboba said with a giggle, we would have to go across the yard to the toilet in the corner of the garden.

I felt privileged to be there, welcomed with open arms into an Afghan home. In the Afghan culture, men who are not immediate family do not mingle with the female members. As a rule, men and women stay in different rooms. That they allowed both Amin and I into the inner spaces of their family life was exceptional.

18

We had visited an Afghan family home once before, in 2006, when Kazem had invited us to his house. Kazem was a calm man who did not reveal much about himself as he drove us around Kabul. We were surprised when, after a few days of spending long hours with him in the car, he casually said that it was the fortieth day since his wife had passed away. Afghans, like Iranians, honour the third, seventh and fortieth days after a person's death. Relatives and friends gather to grieve with the bereaved.

We asked if he wanted the day off. No, he said. He wanted, instead, to invite us to share this ceremony with his family. He had been driving us for several days, silently, patiently, and always with a smile. I never would have guessed that he was concealing the fresh pain of his wife's death.

It seemed to me that, like Kazem, people in Afghanistan generally have a certain poise about concealing their emotions in the face of tragedy. Death and dying, in particular, seem like an easily accepted part of their life. Perhaps if they were to stop and display their feelings, the country would come to a complete standstill: in a place with thirty years of war, filled with orphans and war widows, everyone would have someone to mourn for.

Kazem's house was located on a wide dusty street in an area surrounded by wood-cutters and carpentry workshops. His was a two-storey brick home, a mansion compared to the mud and straw houses we had seen all across Kabul. Kazem and his family were not poor. His wages as a driver for foreign companies, plus the freelance driving he did for the likes of us, must have been bringing in about a thousand dollars a month. In a country where the average income was then less than a hundred Australian dollars a month, Kazem and his family were considered wealthy.

A huge yellow tent was erected in an open space across from the house where the ceremony was to be held. Kazem's friends and family greeted him warmly with hugs and kisses. He introduced us and guided Amin into the tent, a furnace in the summer heat. He took off his shoes and joined some fifty men sitting cross-legged, fanning themselves on the thin red carpet inside, as they read the Qur'an and prayed.

Kazem then accompanied me into the house where the women sat shiva separately. We walked through a garden, past beds of yellow and pink roses, and climbed up a set of metal stairs. The door at the top opened into a cool, light blue corridor with a number of closed doors on each side and a large window at the end, dressed with white curtains. Kazem called out. Several young women in colourful clothes appeared at once from behind different doors, as if expecting me. I felt they were surprised when they saw me, maybe expecting someone older, more mature-looking. Regardless, they greeted me kindly. I had never seen Afghan women in a domestic setting, without their scarves.

I wanted to take their photos as they stood around the hallway, chatting to Kazem. But as soon as I took out my camera they fled, like hens being chased. Kazem laughed. 'They don't like having their pictures taken.' Apologising, I hid my camera.

A blue-eyed blond boy of about eighteen came out of one of the rooms. Ali was Kazem's son. He put his hand across his chest to greet me. He was going to the cemetery to pray for his mother. Did Amin and I want to go with him?

The cemetery was in the foothills of the mountains, overlooked by mud brick houses that huddled on top of one another on the steep slopes. In the red and purple of dusk, the small mounds of earth marked with painted blue stones shone across the land. As far as the eye could see stood these marked unnamed graves.

Only a few variations with deep green flags disrupted the uniformity of the blue mounds on the earth: the martyrs, only those who lost their lives in the path of God, deserved to stand out in death. Ali walked across the mounds and stood next to one with two blue stones. It could have been anyone's. But Ali, and everyone else, knew and remembered exactly where their loved ones were buried. He sat down next to the mound and prayed for his mother. Amin, who had been filming our walk through the darkening cemetery, focused on Ali's face lit purple by the dusk light.

'Why are the graves unmarked?' I asked.

He looked up, his blue eyes reflecting the setting sun. 'What difference does it make? What comes from God goes to God – what difference does it make who lies where? It is only for our own comfort that we furnish and mark the graves. What's important is not how much you decorate or distinguish the grave. This will not help the person go to heaven or be any better. It only makes the ones who are living feel better about themselves when really instead of worshipping the dead and being scared of death and dying, we should try and be kind to the living while we and they are living.'

His words made a lasting impression on me.

19

Waking up after our first comfortable sleep in days, Amin and I washed and went downstairs. We were greeted by the daughters of Mahboba's cousin, who were laying out breakfast. Their mother was making fresh bread, so we went out to watch her. In a sheltered alcove in the garden, she was preparing dough next to a large clay pot by the stairs. She first cleaned out the inside of the pot with a tea towel made from an old shirt, before setting the stove alight. She stretched out pieces of dough on a circular mould and stuck them to the walls of the pot until they turned golden brown, then she flung the baked loaves off using a giant fork, and stored them on a newspaper on the stairs. The bread, served simply with jam, melted in the mouth.

After breakfast, we waited for Mahboba and Virginia. Jameel and Bashir had also joined us, ready to go to Hope House. But there was no sign of the women. Several hours passed. I wrote in my diary. Amin reviewed his footage. The girls went about their daily routine, and Jameel and Bashir lounged on cushions in the sun. The breakfast still lay on the ground, the bread now cold. We were beginning to get worried.

Eventually Virginia and Mahboba came into the room. Virginia's nose was bright red. Mahboba pulled on her hand and told her to sit down for breakfast. One of the girls brought them some fresh tea. Virginia looked at us and chuckled and Mahboba said that Virginia had decided to stay with us for a few more days.

We had not been under the impression that she was to leave.

Then Mahboba turned to Virginia. 'I promise you, just a few days and you will change your mind.'

Virginia replied, more to herself than Mahboba, 'Yes, it will be all right, I guess.'

We soon found out that Virginia had been upset by the numerous travel advisory emails, when news came that an Australian journalist had been killed in Afghanistan. She was feeling so unsafe that she had wanted to call the Australian embassy in Kabul and ask them to help her leave as soon as possible. This had made her feel ill at ease and kept her awake throughout the night. Mahboba had convinced her to stay a few more days. If she seriously felt threatened, she could then go, Mahboba said. But for now we headed to Hope House in the van with the cracked windscreen.

On our way, in the middle of a semi-asphalted major intersection, a burqa-clad woman had spread herself in the mud. Her very small daughter stood next to her. Ahead of us, cars slowed down to avoid them; it was a busy intersection without any traffic lights. The woman put her hand out to every car that passed inches from her. The mud from the tyres was splashing onto the tiny girl's face. She was invisible, almost part of the landscape. Two UN cars drove ahead of us. They did not stop.

As we passed her, Mahboba shouted, 'Jameel, stop! Stop! I want to talk to this woman.'

Jameel stopped right in the middle of the intersection near the woman. None of the other drivers seemed to mind as they manoeuvred around us. Mahboba got out, her bright blue jacket and orange scarf in sharp contrast to the mud-covered woman in a burqa. Amin followed, camera in hand. As did Virginia. I stayed in the van, but I got out my camera and took pictures. Several minutes later they returned.

'I don't believe this,' Virginia said. 'That poor woman and her poor, poor children.'

'Well, that is how it is. She said she has been sitting here every day for weeks and no one ever stops. She has five children. She leaves them alone at home to come and beg. I told her to come to Hope House for Widows' Big Day Out so we can register her to receive basic supplies,' Mahboba said. 'Let's hope she comes.'

'But surely someone must stop to help her?'

'No one does. Everyone is so used to seeing these scenes. You are shocked now. You will be shocked tomorrow. Five days from today, you will not be. You will think it's normal. You will stop seeing them too. This is how it is. When the UN convoys pass, you expect them to help. But all the security, safety, everything is a concern.'

The rest of the trip was silent. I felt a knot in my stomach. Virginia stared out the window.

When we reached Hope House, Virginia immediately checked her email. Mahboba was called to attend a meeting; Amin and I were left in the office with Virginia. Someone brought us a flask of tea. I reviewed some of the photos I had taken. Amin was cleaning mud from his camera.

Virginia turned towards us and said, 'This is ridiculous. They have just sent me another email, warning me not to travel outside of Kabul. For my own safety, they have asked me to report my whereabouts to the Australian embassy here every few days.'

'I want to interview you about this,' Amin said to Virginia. 'Do you mind?'

Virginia teared up and gave a small nervous laugh. 'Sure. Why not?' Amin quickly set himself up.

'I am furious,' she began without any cues from us, 'I am absolutely flabbergasted. In any other country, when a woman sits down on the ground, in the mud, people give a damn. No one gives a damn here. I am in absolute shock at the situation. I can't believe it. It is ridiculous. And to think that a few hours ago, I was ready to call the embassy and leave without even giving myself a chance to understand...'

In the midst of Virginia's emotional outpouring, we were told that Pari had arrived.

Pari was a photographer from Pakistan, Mahboba had told us. I had imagined she would be a plump, short, middle-aged woman, but Palwesha Yusaf was a tall, slim twenty-three-year old with curly black hair. Although she had a Pakistani background, she had grown up in Sydney's inner suburbs. She had been visiting Pakistan, and on her way back to Australia she had come to Kabul. She was a long-time volunteer at Mahboba's Promise, an advocate of peace and human rights, as well as an aspiring photographer, and had travelled to other countries under similar circumstances to learn about the situation on the ground. When we met her, she was encircled by girls who had already befriended her. I realised I had met Pari before. She was the girl behind the computer the first time we had been to Mahboba's office.

Pari, we soon found out, had a great project in mind: she planned to teach the Hope House children some basic photography skills, arm them with cameras, and exhibit their work in Australia.

Pari knew the importance of photography and photojournalism. In a country that was so inaccessible, where so few foreigners dared to come – and those who did were unable to penetrate the deeply segregated and private lives of the locals – photography skills were essential to give the younger generation a means for self-representation and expression. I had seen the importance of this during our previous trip to Afghanistan, especially through the work of Reza Deghati.

20

Reza had been our only contact in Kabul, besides my father, when we arrived in July 2006 to make what became *Hidden Generation*. I had come across him on the Internet while researching for our trip, and emailed him about our idea for the film on women's self-burning. He had replied that he would be delighted to receive us in Kabul.

As soon as we dropped off our bags at the Intercontinental, we asked Kazem to take us to Aina, the media group and training facility Reza had founded with his brother Manoocher. Like other buildings in the Wazir Akbar Khan, Aina too was protected by armed guards stationed in a green container outside its gates. We signed a form and named the person we were to meet, then the underside of our car was inspected with a long mirror for explosives. Beyond the entrance a huge tree-lined square courtyard with a grassy lawn gave us a cool welcome in the July heat. Around the courtyard were a series of rooms, each of which, we soon found out, housed a different department of the Aina network.

There was a radio station, which hosted the first-ever show to air women's voices and issues after the Taliban. Next to it was a newsroom that published a weekly paper, and across from it was the office for *Parvaz*, a glossy educational magazine for children that Reza helped run and distribute. Then there was a visual imaging centre. On the first floor was a photography centre, where Reza and his assistants ran photography workshops for Afghan youth and trained award-winning photographers such as Massud Hosseini. Upstairs were two rooms housing film and editing suites. This was where the first-ever camerawomen of Afghanistan, including Mehr Azizi, were trained and put to work.

Aina was also an open-space gallery. In contrast to the colourless street outside, the walls around the courtyard were filled with large vivid prints of some of Reza's most memorable photos. The exhibition extended into the rooms, with smaller prints in every office and dark hallway.

When Reza came to meet us at the entrance, I recognised him from the pictures I had seen online. He was middle-aged and balding, with a moustache. The deep lines running across his forehead and his protruding nose made him resemble a hawk – a hunter always on the lookout for the best shot. He had deep, kind eyes, and a gaze that showed he was listening with all his attention.

Reza greeted us like family, as if we were returning after years apart. He made us welcome at Aina and encouraged us to use the facilities and make it our base while we were in Kabul. We accepted; Aina became our centre of operations and Reza our guide, helping us turn our idea into reality.

Each afternoon as we drank green tea in the shade of the sycamore trees, after the strain of the day's filming, we were captivated and refreshed by Reza's stories. He told us about his childhood in the city of Tabriz in Iran and his passion for photography, his work on exposing the conditions of the Kurds in Iran which led to his permanent exile from Iran, and his assignments for *National Geographic.* The most compelling was his adventure in seeking out and living with national hero Ahmad Shah Massoud in the mountains of Afghanistan.

After we went back to the Intercontinental each night, Reza would retire to sleep on a thin mattress, half under a desk, in an office space in Aina.

One afternoon, as we sat under the giant image of a young boy holding a flower, Reza brought out several booklets with glossy covers and put them on the glass-topped wicker coffee table. This was *Parvaz*, half in Dari, half in Pashtun. He published it occasionally through Aina and handed copies out to children at orphanages and schools for free. It did not have regular funding and occasional fundraising had only supported about ten issues.

He flipped through the pages and pointed out different sections: one was about science, another world history, and one a themed dictionary in English, Dari and Pashtun. Reza had envisioned *Parvaz*, which in Persian means 'flight', as a book that children could take home from school. Because it was so well printed and durable, he wanted it to be passed around the house to illiterate mothers, sisters and even fathers. It was his way of taking education beyond the school system and into the household.

'But many did not welcome this and instead supported the idea of immediate relief,' he said with a sigh. 'Like giving people fish instead of teaching them how to fish.'

Advertisers were interested but Reza wanted to keep the magazine ad-free. It was a tough choice between publishing regularly and bombarding children with ads, or occasionally but independent of external influences. As he picked up another copy and flipped through it, he said that Coca-Cola, which had recently become popular in Afghanistan, with twenty-metre billboards on the main streets, had offered to support the magazine completely and indefinitely if he would dedicate the inside back cover of every issue to a Coca-Cola ad. After several sleepless nights he had finally made a decision. 'I just couldn't bring myself to do it,' he said. 'I couldn't introduce a new desire to the lives of children and families who barely had clean water to drink.' Since then *Parvaz* had been published only twice, paid for by a well-off Iranian couple in France. But Reza didn't mind.

I really saw the potential of *Parvaz* one morning when we entered the Aina compound to find a sea of children sitting on the green lawn, eating food and drinking carton milk, a rare treat. The children were on an outing from Aschianah, one of Kabul's biggest and oldest orphanages.

After the children watched a performance by three of Reza's friends in clown costumes, joining in the fun and running around the compound, carefree as butterflies, Reza distributed copies of *Parvaz*. There was intense curiosity in the children's faces. Many who had been running wildly now sat down and began to leaf through the pages as they pointed things out to one another.

It became clear to me then why Reza was so proud of this project. I went away that day with an image of illiterate housewives and sisters sitting around in their homes by candlelight as children excitedly narrated to them the images and stories they could not read themselves.

This image only became stronger when we were visiting Kazem's house later in the same trip. We had come back to the house after visiting the cemetery with Ali; it was dark and the last pieces of the yellow tent were being dismantled. Only a few close family members, helping to clean up, remained for dinner.

Upstairs, the men were ushered away, and I was directed into a room full of women which was decorated with gold cushions and lace curtains. My awkward entrance was a distraction for the thirty or so women, who were deep in conversation. I was introduced as the Iranian guest. Two elder aunts shifted heavily and made some space for me. I squeezed in between, feeling everyone's eyes on me. The aunts who sandwiched me smiled and asked what I thought about Afghanistan.

'It is a beautiful place and people are very hospitable,' I said.

By this time everyone was silent and listening to this half-foreigner.

'We love the Iranian accent,' said one of the girls from across the room. 'It is so sweet and crisp.'

I responded, 'I love the Afghan accent because it is original and has less Arabic influence.'

'But your accent sounds more educated,' another girl said.

Another girl from across the room said, 'In Iran

you have a choice to learn how you speak. You can go to school and choose but here there is very little opportunity. Here, for as long as we can remember, there has been war, and we were not sent to school because of it. Then came the Taliban and any chance of education we had, we lost.'

A floodgate opened. Everyone had an opinion. The conversation led me to conclude that most of the women in the room other than the aunties next to me were thirty years old or younger. They remembered nothing but war and fighting. And the majority were illiterate.

One of the girls said her father had hired a Qur'an teacher once a week. But this was not enough. Another young girl who had been silent until then said that her father had enrolled her in school but because the country was still unstable, he had recently pulled her out. 'There are too many risks in going to school,' she said. 'You have to put up with men harassing you on the street as you walk to school. You never know when a suicide bomber might blow up nearby. And to this day, there are some people who would threaten or attack you because they still believe, as the Taliban do, that girls should not go to school.'

Girls had been attacked on their way to school. I later heard about an incident in Kandahar, where the attackers had driven by on a motorcycle and thrown acid at young schoolgirls, leaving several permanently scarred and nearly blinded. That would have been one of the fears of those young women sitting across from me in the dimly lit room.

That night Ali drove us to the Intercontinental. As we headed out, it began to drizzle. Passing by random checkpoints in the dark streets of Kabul, I silently stared through the window. The car was filled with deep, unspoken melancholy. I felt outraged and helpless. I had just left behind nearly thirty capable women who in their whole lives had never formally learned anything, who in the early twenty-first century were still unbelievably and abhorrently uneducated.

I understood what Reza meant when he spoke about taking education beyond the classrooms. I could imagine the women of Kazem's household eagerly listening to how things worked scientifically – how bones were formed, for example, or what stars were made of – and even daring to dream of distant lands like Australia, through copies of *Parvaz*.

That was why when Pari arrived at the Hope House, with so much energy and a brilliant idea to educate and inspire the children, we instantly clicked and started planning the workshops.

Pari had brought with her several donated film cameras. The children loved the idea but equipment and time were limited, so only a few older students were chosen to take part. Because Pari didn't speak Dari, I acted as her interpreter. We taught seven excited teenagers the basics of photography; some had never even held a camera before. Over five or six afternoons they learned about composition, colour, light and the use of shapes, and were given assignments. One day the work was formal, capturing specific shapes or colours, another day it was thematic, focusing on topics such as friendship and love.

Pari would later exhibit the pictures in Australia and the children would prove to be impressive photographers, capturing the intimate details of life boldly and aesthetically, without hesitation. One of the boys got so passionate about photography as a result of this training that he enrolled at Aina, and later became a photographer.

21

We spent about a week helping Pari with the photography training. I came to observe Hope House's different facets through the children's eyes and activities. It was a living microcosm.

With the capacity to sleep just over a hundred children, the three buildings filled with twice that many people during the day, with activities and extracurricular classes, and playgroups. Every morning I watched school-age boys and girls dressed in clean uniforms cram into a minivan with Chinese script on it, and be driven to the local school. When they returned at three o'clock, they had extra classes where they helped each other with homework, learning English, computers and art. We were told the children of Hope House outperform those who live with their families at home. Mahboba has a vision to raise leaders, and she puts a lot of effort into education and bringing up multi-skilled children.

In their photography exercises the children really captured the diversity of life at Hope House. Something they loved to photograph was their peers practising taekwondo. Mahboba had made an impressive effort so that a few times a week, children in crisp donated uniforms gathered in the bright and spacious multipurpose basement of Hope House to learn taekwondo. Here girls and boys were treated equally, and fought against each other. They were so well-practised that they often won medals in inter-club competitions.

I witnessed how these classes benefited the children through Hamid and Hakim, and their older sister, Arezoo. They had been at Hope House for several years by the time we met them. Arezoo was a shy twelve-year-old girl with light hazel eyes and voluminous light brown hair. But her dry skin and the way she smiled, with sadness in her eyes, made her look older. Like every girl at Hope House, her hands and nails were hennaed orange and brown. When we first met her, she blushed and covered her mouth and eyes with her scarf to hide her giggles. On the exterior she was like any normal girl there. A few weeks later, Arezoo and her brothers were the first we interviewed when we thought the wedding was not going to eventuate.

We had set her up in front of the camera, just as we had the other girls and boys. Mahboba asked her to recount the story of how she and her brothers had ended up at Hope House. Her cheeks went red and she held her hand in front of her face.

'My father died of cancer,' she chuckled nervously with her hand still in front of her mouth, 'when Hakim, Hamid and I were very young.' Then she let out a very strange laugh. 'When he died, my mother had nowhere to go, so an auntie in the village decided that she would take us.'

Then her tone changed. She became serious and spoke rapidly. 'Her husband didn't like us to be there. They fought every day, shouting and screaming. But we had nowhere to go and she insisted that we stay. Then one night the fighting got so bad,' she paused, 'he beat her in front us, and then he got a huge knife, and we saw him cut her throat.' She became animated, gesturing with her hands. 'Blood gushing everywhere.'

Everyone in the room froze.

She continued as if in a trance, 'My mother was so scared that she made us grab our things and run out in the middle of the night. We had nowhere to go. We walked for days, until we reached another village where we had some family. They had a farm and cattle. My mother left us there. The family used my brothers as shepherds. They were very little, maybe five or six then. One day when a wolf ate the cattle dog and then a sheep, the wife was so angry that she locked up my brothers in the outdoor toilet, not allowing anyone else in the household to use it.

'For three days and nights my brothers cried inside the toilet. I tried to beat her up to force her to release them, but I wasn't strong enough. She didn't feed them. I took them some bread, but she grabbed it from me, threw it on the ground and stamped her feet on it. I slept outside the toilet every night to keep them company. Then after three days, she decided to let them out. When she did, they bolted, ran and ran, but they had nowhere to go. They had to come back.

We had nowhere to go. So we had to stay until our mother came to pick us up again much later. But again, we had nowhere to go. We finally heard of this place, and she left us here…'

With the last sentence, some kind of a floodgate opened in her body. She let out a grunt, and started making noises as if she was gasping for air. It was hard to tell whether she was laughing or sobbing. When Mahboba tried to comfort her, Arezoo continued to wail loudly, so she reached out and held her tightly in her arms, and the two of them wept, one louder than the other. Arezoo continued to cry, even after the children left the room, even after we stopped filming. For several days she shook and had outbursts of emotion. Mahboba took extra care of her, monitoring her by keeping her close, even taking her to the cousin's house to sleep for a few nights.

Arezoo became very special to Amin and me. We had been warned against getting too close to the children, because of our inevitable departure. But we were both getting inextricably attached to Arezoo. After the interview, during the few days that she spent travelling in the van with us, watching Amin and me work, she became our friend. She played games with Amin, jumping in front of the camera or suddenly hugging him. She would volunteer to carry my camera bag, hold my hand, and walk with me wherever I went in Hope House. It was like we had become the big brother and sister she never had. Over the time that we were there, she became almost inseparable from us. She would retreat to her room when we left to go to the cousin's house at night. We were uneasy about this, knowing it would make things hard when we had to leave. I also began to sense a tinge of jealousy from some of the other girls. I tried to balance this by spending time and playing with them, or letting them bring me tea and carry my bag, which was their way of showing affection.

Since Mahboba had arrived, the children didn't pile up each day to watch soap operas. Instead, they gathered in the common room, danced and played games. Mahboba was usually very playful. The children put make-up on her, massaged her, brushed her hair and brought her tea. On one of those nights, when the children were happily playing or dancing to the rhythmic sound of the frame drum, I noticed

Arezoo looked upset and left the room. After a few minutes, when she didn't return, I sought her out and found her in her room, crying. Since we had done the interview, I thought it was a good opportunity to follow up this conversation on film. I called Amin out, trying not to let any of the other kids notice we had slipped out. Camera in hand, we went to Arezoo's room, where she was on her bed sobbing.

I sat next to her and she stopped crying. As Amin set up his camera, I asked her what was wrong. At first, she said nothing. Then she began to sob again. After some silence, she told me that the music reminded her of her mother, who used to play the instrument while the three children danced. I didn't know what to say, so instinctively I hugged her tightly. Her heart was beating fast as she put her rough, calloused hands around me. Amin, who had been behind the camera until then, came and sat on her other side, and we hugged her between us. She closed her eyes. Her heart slowed down. I have no idea how long we sat there on the bed, in the dim room lit by only one flimsy light. It could have been ten minutes or an hour. Arezoo eventually fell asleep in our arms and we tucked her in.

When we went back to the common room, the children asked us where we had been. Without giving a clear answer, we pretended to be happy and played with them again, but neither of us could really enjoy the moment.

Several days later, we saw Arezoo at taekwondo practice. The aggression that she let out, the fight she put up, was incredible. She didn't give up. She beat all the boys, even those older and bigger than her.

A few days later again, we were invited to watch a taekwondo competition. We huddled into the van with the team. All the way, Mahboba cheered, singing songs of victory. Although this was a boys-only event, Mahboba had asked Arezoo to come along. She was the only girl and was not to fight, but she still wore her combat gear, and a yellow and white knitted beanie that covered her lush hair.

The club where the fight was to take place was in the basement of a newly finished building, but the street in front of it, like any other side street in Kabul, was unasphalted. We only had to take a few steps from the van to the entrance, but even then, we got mired in mud and the fresh white pants of the boys' uniforms got stained. We took off our shoes and went down the dark stairway to the club. The large mirrors that covered one side of the room made it look brighter and larger than it was. Coaches, referees and supporters of the other teams greeted us warmly.

We sat down on chairs lined up especially for us. Our team was quickly rounded up by their coach for warm-up. Gradually other teams trickled into the basement and each huddled into a corner. Tension was building up in the room as the last team arrived and the organisers announced the order of the fights. Amin had already begun to film; Pari and I, with one of the boys learning photography, took pictures of the boys in their warm-up. As I photographed Arezoo and Mahboba sitting at the back of the room together, Arezoo looking nervous and Mahboba chatting with one of the coaches, I realised our team was the only one to have brought female supporters, and a girl dressed to fight.

The opponent teams were clearly from well-off families. Most Afghan families, struggling to make ends meet, didn't have spare cash for children's sport.

As the games began, our group was referred to by the organisers as 'the Orphanage Team'. Mahboba cringed every time. But as it turned out, our team, with the least equipment, training and facilities, was outperforming everyone else. By the halfway mark, we had won several medals.

The big fight everyone had been waiting for was between Hakim and a boy from one of the high-class clubs who walked to the mat and took a bow with a smug expression on his face. It was a tense fight. When Hakim hit the floor, Arezoo's face wrinkled. The boys fought powerfully for several minutes, until the referee called out Hakim for a foul. Our team members shouted that it was an unfair call, but he didn't listen. Within a few seconds, Hakim took a blow to the shin and fell. He didn't stay down. Limping, he continued, taking hits left and right. And then he fell and couldn't get up. He tried, but it was impossible. Our coach ran to him, followed by some of the boys. Arezoo sprang across the room, pushed everyone aside and held her brother's hand, whispering to him. He was holding back tears, his face red. For the winner, this match would bring a coveted gold medal, and could have put Hope House at the top of the rankings.

I went closer to listen to Arezoo and Hakim. He

was staring beyond her with teary eyes. She shook him by the shoulders and he looked up at her. She was telling him not to continue because it would injure him and he would lose the chance to compete in other events. For a moment he considered his big sister's words very seriously. Mahboba walked over and told him not to worry, it was not a big deal. He had already brought in many gold medals.

The referees needed to move on – would he continue to fight or not? Then Arezoo shouted out, 'I will continue the fight on his behalf.' Mahboba followed loudly, 'Yes! let her do it!' There was silence.

Hakim's opponent, who was standing casually in a corner, stood up straight. The men in charge whispered amongst themselves. Our coach went over to talk to them. A few minutes passed and they reached a conclusion: with great apologies to Mother Mahboba, they could not allow Arezoo to fight. It was against the rules. The person who started the round should finish it. As the result of Hakim forfeiting the match, his opponent received the gold medal. For the rest of the competition, Arezoo remained on the mats with her brothers and the other boys.

Back at Hope House, an excited crowd of boys

and girls welcomed the champions. The boys who had fought, including Hakim, who was still upset for his loss, wore their medals proudly around their neck for a while before handing them to Mahboba to display in the office next to dozens of others they had already won.

Although we never had the opportunity to see the girls' competition, they had also won medals and gained strength through taekwondo. Maryam, a fourteen-year-old Hazara girl, was shy but witty. She had grown in confidence through the sport.

She had come to Hope House in the early years of Mahboba's Promise, when Mahboba had still personally looked for children on the streets and in the camps. On a hot summer day Mahboba and her office attendant were walking around the shantytowns on the outskirts of Kabul looking for those most in need. Among the tents in the foul-smelling landscape Mahboba saw a tiny girl all alone, playing with rubbish. She looked frail and unwell, black with dirt, and flies stuck to her face. When Mahboba enquired about the child's mother, they found her searching another pile of refuse for food. Mahboba offered to take care of Maryam in a beautiful new building with good facilities; the mother accepted with gratitude.

Maryam smelled so pungent that they had to open the car windows as they drove her to Hope House. She was scrubbed seven times before all the grit and dirt was cleaned properly and her true skin colour showed through.

Maryam really started to blend in with the other children after starting to practise taekwondo. It made her physically stronger, and the medals had given her a sense of confidence that I could see in all her interactions.

22

Besides taekwondo, many other activities took place at Hope House. It was through watching these I noticed that the core of Mahboba's work was to empower children and women through education, so that they could eventually take care of themselves. In a country where women could engage in very few public and paid positions back then, Mahboba was focused on teaching skills they could practise from the safety of their own homes.

The Sewing Centre, funded by the Australian government, was a vital part of life at Hope House. When we visited it one afternoon, a woman was cutting patterns from newspapers with a chunky pair of scissors; another was smoothing out the creases of a shawl with a heavy metal iron, occasionally topping up her equipment from a supply of burning coal in a corner of the room; others were hemming on pedal-operated gold and black Singer sewing machines that were always reliable, since they did not depend on Afghanistan's failing electricity.

One of the teachers greeted us. Conscious of the camera and Mahboba's presence, he proudly explained that the women were in the last stages of the course, having learned a range of skills. He picked up samples of baggy tops and pants hung on crude metal frames placed around the room to showcase the women's work.

Mahboba had organised for the women to produce a large number of small soft dolls, which were to be sold as part of a Mahboba's Promise campaign in Australia. These simple miniature dolls with white cotton faces and a few quick stiches for their eyes and mouths, were lined up on the windowsill, dressed in red and green clothes, and had their heads covered with matching scarves.

Mahboba picked one up and said to me in English, 'Look, they are so sad. They are all frowning.' She then turned to the teacher and the students, 'Can you make them smile? Just sew the mouth upwards not downwards. No one wants to buy sad dolls in Australia.'

'What can we do, sister?' the teacher laughed. 'That's what I told them before too. This is how they feel.'

In a room across from the Sewing Centre, on the ground floor of Hope House, Mahboba had established a beauty school. Usually men are not allowed to enter women's beauty salons, but because Mahboba wanted him to document the centre, Amin was able to walk in with Pari, Virginia and me, hiding behind his camera.

This room was painted light pink and covered with clippings of women's hairstyles from Western magazines, though what the women learned bore no resemblance to what was on the walls. What they had studied, and prepared to show Mahboba on the day we visited, was their graduating projects of bridal make-up.

As we entered, students were carefully putting finishing touches on two model 'brides'. The teacher proudly greeted us and asked the brides to turn around. One of the women was Hanieh, a teenager with smooth light skin, now unrecognisable. Her honey-brown eyes were hidden under heavy false lashes and the bright pink and blue eye shadow that was splattered around her lids. Her lips had been drawn on larger than life with mauve lipstick. Her cheeks were pink. Her hair was covered with a wig of curls, topped with a plastic tiara and a veil hanging in the back. She was wearing a long-sleeved white wedding dress.

The other model had a different look. In a sleeveless wedding dress and a wig of dark brown braids, she self-consciously held her arms across her bare shoulders. Her dark eyes had been highlighted with bright blue and green shades and were heavy with diamanté-studded fake lashes. Like Hanieh, she, too, had pink cheeks and huge red lips.

Pari and I hid behind our cameras to avoid showing any kind of reaction; we didn't understand that what would be considered theatrical by Western beauty standards was seen as incredibly beautiful by the Afghan fashion trends of the time. Virginia's smiles, gestures and expression of sheer surprise were misread as emphatic approval. The women became insistent on giving her a makeover. A quick look at the colourful palettes of eye shadow scattered on the table, the unwashed, reused brushes, and the blunt pencils and lipsticks that had been used so much that the last remaining pigment could only be fished out with cotton buds, was enough to make her refuse. But the women sat her down almost forcefully on a broken chair.

Caught out, Virginia was a good sport. Smiling for the camera, the face of ABC Canberra News was transformed into an Afghan bride. Pink and blue eye shadow almost reached her eyebrows; her cheeks were painted bright pink and her lips were outlined with a blunt pencil and filled in with a used-up lipstick. She firmly refused the mascara, claiming an allergy. Finally, her hair was clipped with a large braid. Luckily for Virginia, she could not leave the room like that and the make-up was quickly wiped off.

Owning a salon had become lucrative business for women, as I had witnessed during our trips to Afghanistan. In March 2006 we had seen few publicly advertised beauty salons, but by July every street corner had a salon, each identified by a banner bearing oversized hand-painted portraits of women's faces with extravagant make-up, and a name like 'Heart of the Bride', 'The Bride's Day' and 'Love of the Bride'. On this trip, three years later, I had noticed even more of them. Those who successfully made it in the budding beauty business in Afghanistan, we were told, were in good shape.

But there was a downside to this business. Given Afghanistan's conservative nature, it was still not accepted for women to be involved in what was deemed a frivolous and un-Islamic activity. The Taliban had until recently forbidden women from doing innumerable things, including wearing make-up and tending to their beauty. Although the Taliban were no longer officially in power, they were never too far away. That is why only four women were enrolled in that year's beauticians' course, compared to a dozen in tailoring, which was seen as a safe activity. Mahboba even worried that running the beautician course could jeopardise Hope House: if people thought that it was leading women towards corruption, it could make the centre a target of attacks. The course was discontinued the following year.

I saw the impact of both these courses on the

women's lives a few days later when on a rainy day, dozens of women, their relatives and friends gathered to celebrate their first step towards self-sufficiency at the graduating ceremony in the basement of Hope House.

As the women came up to receive their certificates and take photos under banners reading 'Mahboba's Promise Sewing Centre Graduation' – which included the beautician course – next to mannequins displaying their work, they blushed, giggled and hid their faces with their hands and scarves. For many, this would be the first and only time they would be recognised semi-publicly for any achievement. What added to the excitement was not the piece of paper – which many couldn't even read and which was essentially useless since they couldn't use it to gain any sort of employment – but that each graduating woman was given her own Singer sewing machine with threads, some fabric and other equipment. This prize could mean the difference between starvation and life. The faces of the women graduating from both courses were bright with hope.

Hanieh was exuberant. We had seen her around Hope House, usually looking dejected. She had told us about herself in an interview. She was the eldest of three daughters in a family whose only source of income was their ailing father, who sold phone cards on the street. The fact that they didn't have a brother jeopardised their lives; because their father didn't have sons or other protectors who could take care of his territory, he was often bullied and pushed out of his work zone. This left them with little income. Hanieh wanted her sisters and herself to go to school. But that was impossible. She was depressed and often contemplated suicide. Many times, she told me in the interview, she had thought about jumping in front of a truck. The only reason she didn't do it was that she didn't want to put her mother through grief.

On graduation day, Hanieh was excited. I saw her mother in the audience with her sisters when she was receiving her certificate. We hugged her after the ceremony, elated at her new-found hope.

23

In 2006, on a hot July day in the midst of the work on our film about women in despair, I had spent a morning at Aina talking to a woman who had found hope, though it had come with a whole new layer of trouble. It was the day before we were to film in a hospital burns unit.

Mehr Azizi was a tough twenty-year-old with a deep vertical frown line running down her forehead, a reminder of the tragedy she encountered as a child. Early one morning her mother had risen for her dawn prayers. Like every other day, she had silently gone to the spare room on the top floor of their suburban Kabul home. Without any warning, a bomb was dropped nearby and the force of the blast caused the roof of their house to collapse. They woke up to the explosion, and looked for their mother, only to find her half-buried under the rubble. Mehr hugged her, keeping her calm, while her father and the other children called for help. She died in the arms of her thirteen-year-old daughter, leaving behind not only pain and sorrow in Mehr's heart, but also the responsibility for a household of several younger siblings and an ailing father who had just retired. Housebound under the Taliban, instead of going to school, Mehr mothered her young brothers and sisters.

When she was sixteen, soon after the Taliban was ousted, Mehr heard of a course run by Aina. For the first time in the history of Afghanistan, girls were being trained as camerawomen. She proposed the idea to her father. He rejected it and told her never to speak about it again. She mentioned it to her older brother who reacted the same way. But Mehr was determined and despite their objection she enrolled herself in the course, alongside a few other brave girls. Together they worked their way through a series of practical workshops run by a foreign, non-Muslim team. This not only secured Mehr a job as a video journalist at Aina, which provided for her family, but it also led to the production of the revolutionary film *Afghanistan Unveiled*, which documented the lives of rural Afghan women in regions formerly controlled by the Taliban, such as Bamiyan. This was a courageous act, considering that in late 2002, less than a year after the fall of the Taliban, the country was still unsettled and many women feared even leaving their homes in suburban Kabul. Following the success of the film, Mehr had travelled to Canada and some European countries to promote it.

But she was bearing the consequences of her courage, she told me as we lounged on low cushions in Aina's light-filled media suite, where a rusty ceiling fan swirled too slowly to cool the hot July day. In a still-traditional country where men preferred women to stay at home and definite rules existed about believers and unbelievers, her public appearance and close friendship and association with non-Muslim people through Aina had jeopardised her safety and that of her family. While her father and brother were barely on speaking terms with her, she regularly received calls threatening her and her siblings' lives. Her neighbours called out offensive names to her brothers for letting their sister roam free, and were the subjects of regular street fights. Her fears had intensified when in 2005, Shaima Rezayee, the first female Afghan TV presenter for a pop music show, was shot dead in her Kabul home at the age of twenty-four by religious conservatives.

After telling me all of this and settling into an eerie silence, she sighed. 'When I step out of these doors every day I have no idea if I will ever make it home alive or not.'

I had no idea what to say. The silence lay heavily between us.

After a few moments, I reminded her that we wanted to interview her for her opinion on the recent increase in women's self-burning.

She nodded, then asked if we had the right permissions to film. I showed her a permit we had from Foreign Affairs. She looked at it and, speaking from experience, said that if we wanted to film inside government-run facilities, particularly hospitals, we would need an authorisation letter from the Ministry of Health. They would be more likely to welcome us if we came with a letter, so it would be worthwhile to obtain one.

We were planning to film at the Kabul Istiqlal Hospital the following day. As we sat there, sipping green tea, and Mehr was lost in her own world, I thought perhaps I could get the permit. When I suggested this, she told me that the Ministry of Health was not too far away – less than ten minutes by taxi.

I considered it. It would be very helpful to have that piece of paper the next day, but I also feared wandering into the city on my own. I did speak the language so there was no fear of getting lost or caught out. I had ventured into the streets with Amin almost every day since we had arrived. It was a relatively safe time in Afghanistan, so the chances of getting caught up in crossfire or a bombing were not high. I convinced myself that my fear was unfounded and had more to do with stepping beyond my comfort zone than any real danger.

Mehr saw me out to the street and helped me get a taxi. I found the Ministry of Health, a run-down brown building with endless corridors, showed my permit, got a form and was sent away to get it signed at Istiqlal Hopsital.

I didn't know where the hospital was but was told

a taxi driver would. Confident now in navigating the city by myself, I hailed a taxi. Fifteen minutes later, it stopped in front of the hospital on a wide unpaved road. A warm wind was blowing heavy dust, and women in blue burqas looked like birds on the ground, flapping their wings desperately. The city had a sepia filter; even the burqas seemed drained of their colour. The hospital was protected by tall walls and a huge blue door.

Mehr's advice had given me confidence to take a huge step. What I would see inside would make me realise the importance of the work that people like Reza were doing for the women and children of Afghanistan. It would change my life and be the cause that would eventually bring me back to Kabul and Hope House. And it would later be one of the main reasons that I persisted with the telling of the stories in this book.

24

For days after Pari's arrival at Hope House, we occupied ourselves with her photography project and playing with the children as the wedding continued to stall.

It was during this time that I had the epiphany about writing the story of the encounters I had in Afghanistan through the film we were making and the one we had already made. It happened just after an interview with one of the girls, Monireh, on the day we were interviewing the children.

As she sat in front of the camera, Monireh continually twisted the corners of her red scarf between her forefinger and thumb. I knew Monireh. I had played with her and some of the other girls the day before. She had darker skin and was much taller than her peers. She reminded me of a gazelle, with her liquid brown eyes and long light sprints across the playground. Like most of the other children here, she appeared to be healthy and happy. No one suspected that beneath her composed and sometimes audacious exterior there was deep trauma, well hidden, waiting to erupt.

I held my breath in anticipation of another story. Now, in front of the camera, gaze down, after casually telling us how her father had died and she and her mother had been left at the mercy of an uncle, she said, 'One day, when I was nine or ten, and I got home without any money after a day of pretending to be retarded and knocking on car windows for spare change, my uncle pushed me to the floor and beat me. He pulled live electric cords from the wall and gave me a shock. I still remember the feeling of the current going through my body. I couldn't move. Thinking that I might die, he began to whip the soles of my feet with the wire… I could hear my mother shouting in the background…and then…nothing.'

With those words the world around me darkened. I threw the microphone onto the floor, ruining the sound. I heard myself let out a loud uncontrollable shrill, and when I came to my senses I was in the middle of the room, tightly hugging Monireh and sobbing. We stood there – a twenty-eight-year-old Iranian-Australian woman, and a twelve-year-old Afghan girl – held tightly in each other's arms, accompanied by a choir of weeping girls, for what felt like eternity.

This moment of madness was a turning point for me. A lump of sorrow, of unsaid words, had grown in my throat by the time I heard Monireh's story. When I escaped onto the roof to take a breath, I knew that if these children could not shout beyond this room, I could. I must.

While Mahboba tended to other tasks, we became immersed in the life of Hope House. I began to note in detail the stories I was encountering, as we anticipated some news that would move the wedding forward. But each day women and young girls recruited to find a wife for Fatemeh's brother brought news of rejections. And then, among the women graduating from the tailoring course, Mahboba spotted a potential match for Fatemeh's brother.

Sameera was a young girl of about seventeen with curly black hair, which she covered loosely with a scarf. I had seen her in Hope House. She was animated, wilful and street smart, and liked by everyone. She lived across the street with her mother and sisters, and spent her days helping around Hope House. After the graduation ceremony, with one less project on her plate, and with time running out, Mahboba decided to take matters into her own hands and go to their house the day after to propose.

The next day, however, a heavy rain nearly flooded Hope House, forcing us to cancel the proposal plans. The rain turned the office managers' attention to the shipping container sitting behind the basketball court which they feared could also have flooded.

This big box, we were told, held shoes. During the time we had been at Hope House, I had observed the children and their clothing. While they were well dressed, in clean clothes, I would see children on the playground shoed in whatever they could find: one slipper on one foot and none on the other, or shoes from different pairs on each foot. Sometimes they wore nothing on their feet at all. Seddiq always complained when he saw them in mismatched shoes. It was not like they didn't have any, he once told me, but what they had was often misplaced among the group, or worn out too soon. This carelessness had left Hope House in shoe crisis.

When the rain subsided, Seddiq and Abdul Fattah went to open the container. The children huddled behind the basketball court fences, curiously peering out. In a show of manners everyone kept their distance until hundreds of pairs of shoes had been brought out, and the older students, following instructions from Abdul Fattah and Seddiq, laid them out. Four to five rows of basketball shoes, trainers, flats, Crocs, boots, colourful sandals, and dress shoes, in different sizes, filled the entire length of the nearly-ten-metre path leading from the playground to the office. Once the container had been emptied out, Abdul Fattah commenced the allocation.

My heart ached, watching this process. There was no choice for these children. Everyone was lined up to their height. Abdul Fattah picked out a pair that looked like it would fit the child in front of him, and let them try it. It could be anything: tennis shoes, Crocs, even summer sandals. If the shoes were too small, he would choose another pair; too big, he would let them go – the child would grow into them. I could see children eyeing certain pairs, hoping that by luck they would get their choice. Some did. Others did not, and reluctantly accepted whatever was given to them. Some boys ended up with pink-laced girls' tennis shoes, some girls with tough boots. No one complained.

Once the shoes had been handed out, boys and girls huddled together, showing each other what luck had brought them. Some exchanged pairs among themselves. Others, happy with what they had been given, put them on and went back to doing whatever they had been doing earlier, only this time in matching shoes. Seddiq, standing next to me, predicted that this would last two days. He wasn't wrong. Two days later, everyone, again, wore mismatched shoes. There was nothing anyone could do.

Shoes had taken up the entire cloudy morning. It started to pour again in the afternoon. We decided to postpone Sameera's proposal again to avoid the mud.

The following afternoon, we headed to Sameera's house across the street. A car, then a truck stirred up the fine dust that had now replaced the mud, blocking our visibility. Mahboba, Virginia, Amin and I coughed it out and continued.

On the way, Mahboba told me Sameera's story. When she was small, just after her sister was born, her father died of cancer. He left them nothing. Sameera, her older sister and their mother, along with their new-born baby sister were left on the street. During the day, they separated and begged across town, with a baby in tow. For a few months, they survived on discarded rotting fruit and vegetables. Then a family friend told them about Mahboba's Promise. They made it to one of Mahboba's open days for widows, and signed up to receive basic supplies. Soon, they were sponsored by someone in Australia and moved across the street to a house like the one in which Fatemeh and her father lived. Mahboba's Promise rented houses in the vicinity of Hope House and subsidised the rent for impoverished families until they could sustain themselves. The family managed to gain their independence as the sisters learned sewing and started to make simple garments for women in the area.

This house was one of those brick ones the owner

of which had long ago run out of money to finish. Sameera's family lived in the doorless front room, separated from the hallway by a blanket. The back was rented to another widow and her young children. The two families shared an alcove where they did their cooking. There was no running water or gas. Only a broken cabinet tilting forward, several pieces of distorted and misshapen cookware, and a single portable picnic gas cylinder, which I knew to be a seriously dangerous apparatus since my trip to the women's burns unit, made up their kitchen.

Their room smelt musky and was furnished with a few cushions to one side, a rough rug on the floor, and a china cabinet housing some chipped dishes. Their bedding was piled up in a corner and covered with a white sheet. The room had not been painted yet. The white plaster looked damp. We were told it leaked during the rainy season. We were guided in and settled ourselves against thc cushions; Amin set up the camera, and I the sound equipment.

Mahboba got straight to the point. 'As you know, we are trying to marry Abdul Fattah and Fatemeh.' Abdul Fattah blushed ear to ear. 'But her father wants us to find his son a bride before he will allow the marriage to take place. We have come to ask for your daughter's hand in marriage to him.'

Sameera and her older sister were absent from the room. It was up to their mother to make a decision. She was a shy woman, probably in her late thirties, who covered her mouth as she spoke softly. She sat next to the china cabinet, with her knees folded into her chest and covered with her long dress. With her little daughter in front of her, she stared at the floor for a few seconds before responding.

'I can't do that. My daughters are very young. I want them to be educated. She just graduated from the tailoring course, so we finally have someone to help us.'

'I understand your concern. But Fatemeh's brother is a good boy from a good family. I have known you for so long, I only want what is best for the girls,' Mahboba responded.

A few inaudible words followed, before she repeated, 'No doubt. But I want my daughters to be educated. They are too young. I don't know his family that well. You know how it works here. Reputations and how well you know someone are very important.'

An uncomfortable silence followed. Amin intervened. 'Can the girls come in?'

The mother blushed. 'No, no,' she said, 'that's not possible.'

Awkward glances darted around the room. Mahboba broke the silence, looking at me and Amin. 'Okay. Let's go, then. Let's go look elsewhere.' On her cue everyone got up and filed out. As we walked back towards Hope House, Virginia wanted to know what had happened. Mahboba repeated the conversation.

'But Mahboba,' Virginia said, 'don't you feel weird doing this? Coming to someone's house and asking for their daughter's hand in marriage for a boy you have never met? You know that anywhere else in the world this would be… unacceptable.'

'Yes, I understand that. But here it is accepted. If you have a daughter, you can expect someone to knock on the door and say that they want to marry your daughter.'

Virginia's lips twisted. 'But…'

'This is the tradition here, we have no other choice. This is the way things are done.'

I could see that Virginia couldn't identify with this tradition. But for now it was left at that. 'What are we going to do now?'

'Look for another girl. But I'm not sure how we

are going to do that. We don't have much time left,' Mahboba replied.

We had already been in Kabul over two weeks. We had not yet met Fatemeh, her father or her brother, the 'good' boy for whom we were trying to find a wife.

25

With days left before we all had to return to Australia, I was worried, more than anything else, about Fatemeh's future and well-being. We didn't see any clear path forward as to where we would find the right woman for her brother in the short time we had left. One morning, when all leads had failed, as Amin and I sat in the office working, Virginia asked me whether or not we might be able to find a suitable woman at the upcoming Widows' Big Day Out.

Mahboba, who was listening, jumped in, surprised. 'Well, that's not possible. They don't want a widow.'

'Why not? What if we don't call her a widow?'

'Well, a widow is a widow, you know… They want a virgin…' Mahboba responded awkwardly.

'Ohhh, right.'

This was not a bad idea. Had this been an option, we would have found a very suitable and willing wife for Fatemeh's brother as soon as we wanted. Many widows, young and old, frequented Hope House. Every month hundreds of women lined up on the grounds to collect small rations of rice, oil, flour and green tea.

Once every several years, Mahboba combined this with what she called Widows' Big Day Out. I had heard about this event from Mahboba, who had proudly recounted its success. On this day, everyone who was sponsored was invited to come along and to bring anyone who might be in need. A few years before, Widows' Big Day Out had attracted two thousand women. Mahboba expected a similar turnout this time.

I felt fortunate that we were in Kabul at a time when such an event was to take place and yet I had not prepared myself for how emotionally charged it would be. The preparations for the day took a lot out of Mahboba and her team. It also redirected us for a few days from pursuing the wedding plans.

Mahboba insisted that the day was not about

getting women to the premises for handouts. She wanted to involve them and give them the opportunity to enrol in various courses and activities to develop income-producing skills such as sewing and crafts, areas that had proved successful at various Mahboba's Promise charity events in Australia. Embroidered shawls, cushion covers and even pyjamas had been well received. Mahboba wanted to engage and recruit women to continue their production. However, she did not have the means to support this initiative on a large scale at Hope House. As she had with many other projects, she chose to partner with a successful group that managed the stores and workshops at Women's Park.

Women's Park was a desolate space in the centre of Kabul, designated solely for women. I had been to the park in 2006 when we were making *Hidden Generation*. Amin had waited outside while I passed a few security checkpoints and crossed into what I had imagined would be a garden full of lush trees and shade, a private sanctuary where women could easily take off their covers, get some sun on their skin and wind through their hair. But with plots of barren land, a few swings and broken-down play equipment, the park was a depressing site.

While the park didn't offer women the experience of my Australian imagination, it did offer something much more vital: the promise of a livelihood. Back then this was one of the few places in Afghanistan where women could work in shops. All across the park, women ran successful businesses making and selling crafts, including embroidery, clothing and jewellery. Catering mostly to foreign visitors and better-off Afghan women who could afford the luxury of coming to a park with family and friends, the women sold their attractively presented stock well above the average market price. The organisation that managed the park also ran courses and provided work opportunities.

When I visited it again in 2009 with Mahboba, in preparation for the Widow's Day Out, the park was greener and more shops were in operation. It appeared to have grown, and more women were also engaged in courses. In a small assembly line, we saw women welding together locally made electronic items. In another room they were creating simple, elegant necklaces and earrings. Some of this jewellery was displayed and sold in the park itself, while other pieces were taken to uptown hotels and sold to foreigners, who found them affordable despite their inflated prices.

The woman who organised the courses, wearing a loose cream shawl around her head and a long brown jacket, appeared sturdy and strong. She was obviously in charge. After showing us around the compound and the various activities, she had agreed to come and introduce the available opportunities to the women at the Big Day Out.

Now, women of all ages were trickling into Hope House for the Widows' Big Day Out. Over the course of the day, about three thousand would pass through the doors. By the time we arrived at around nine, the entire grounds were a blue sea of women, with invisible children tagging along under their mothers' burqas. We were told they had begun to arrive as early as seven-thirty, camping in clusters. Many had travelled long distances to get there. By eleven the compound was completely packed.

Our mission was to document the day. Pari, Virginia and I were given instructions to photograph, and Amin to film. We positioned ourselves to cover as much of the place as we could. We could barely move in the dense crowd.

When Seddiq began to guide the women into the basement, three hundred or so crammed in, squashing against one another. I flowed down the stairs in the river of blue. It was a cool day outside but the basement quickly heated up. I was pushed into a corner, and stayed where I landed. There was no room to take even a few steps. The older girls brought in kettle after kettle of green tea, plates of biscuits, cups, and small cartons of milk for the women, many of whom may not have had a proper meal in days. After the women had eaten, Mahboba made her entrance to applause and cheering. She stood by the door where there was a tiny bit of space and began to speak.

'Hope House is here to help you,' she said, as the women listened intently. 'We want to help you, but we don't want to provide you with charity. I am not going to give you money every month. If you think that, go look elsewhere. What I want is to teach you skills so that you can bring in income. So you can feed your children, hold your heads up high and be proud of yourselves.'

'But sister, we have no skills, and who would take care of our children when we come to learn?' one woman shouted.

'That's no problem. That is why I am going to teach you skills. As for the children, bring them here, they can play with the other children and have a meal while you attend classes.'

'What kind of skills?'

'Sisters, there are so many things you can learn. You can learn to sew, make handicrafts and jewellery, even become a beautician. I run these courses for you for free but you have to promise to attend regularly. I would like to show you what I mean.'

Mahboba then invited the Women's Park course co-ordinator to talk. She held up samples of crafts. She explained that they might look complicated but they were not. Other women, just like them, had learned to make them, step by step.

'It takes about six months for you to complete a course, but even after that we support you. We will buy your products and sell them for you. If you feel confident, we can even help you set up your own shop in your own area, or in the park. We want to support you, but you also need to be persistent.'

The women whispered among themselves.

Mahboba continued where the co-ordinator had left off. 'You see these?' She held out of one the frowning dolls. 'People in Australia will buy them. Your work can go across the oceans and into someone's house. Someone will buy it and put it in their house and look at it and say how talented Afghan women are.'

I continued to photograph the women's reactions.

'Imagine: you learn these things and then your children will no longer be hungry. You will not depend on anyone,' Mahboba said.

Murmurs were still going on.

Then the co-ordinator took over again. 'If you are interested, come see me and we can help you get started.'

'Enjoy the rest of your time here,' Mahboba concluded. 'Go upstairs and look around the Sewing Centre. We also have the clinic which is opening today. This is a free service for you and your children. You can go to the doctor and tell him what is ailing you and your family. Don't forget that we also have a chance to find you a sponsor. But you have to go to the office to register. Then I will go to Australia and look for kind people to support you. This can provide you with basic food supplies and some schooling gear for your children until you find your own footing. May God be with all of you.'

Then Mahboba left the basement, giving me a contented smile on her way. Some women followed her, others stayed behind to talk to each other.

Outside of the basement, Mahboba was immersed in a group of women. I stood close to her, photographing and watching her as she moved gracefully through the crowd. She listened to every woman compassionately and with total presence. Women she passed clutched at her and kissed her face and hands. Mahboba knew many of them by name, and knew their harrowing stories.

One woman stood out of the crowd, wearing a bright pink scarf. When Mahboba saw her, she was overcome with joy. They kissed and hugged like old friends. Mahboba pulled Virginia and me aside, and told us her story.

The woman in pink had wizened skin with deep lines on her forehead. She looked like an elderly woman but was probably no older than forty. She had lost some of her front teeth, and there was a great depth of sadness in her dark eyes. During the Taliban, on her way to the shops, she had been kidnapped by a group of men and held captive in a dark cell where she was blindfolded, tied to a pole and continuously gang-raped. She did not know how long she was held, when she was eventually released. After a few months, her family had given up. They were surprised to see her turn up at the door, the living dead. Somehow, she had managed to survive the horror, but her body still bore the pain. I watched Virginia's face transform as she heard this story, from curiosity to horror and then sadness and pain. She controlled herself and hid her eyes behind her camera.

I was standing close to the woman. She looked at me and smiled with kind eyes. My heart was beating rapidly and my palms were sweaty from her story. I knew I couldn't look at her without breaking down if I allowed my heart to even touch the edges of her experience. I returned a quick smile, busied myself by taking more pictures, and quickly moved on.

Women filed in and out of Hope House all day.

Mahboba was floating around like a buoy, carried whichever way by the wave of women. I followed her. By two in the afternoon she looked utterly overwhelmed. We had all skipped lunch, and Mahboba was starting to look very pale as women continued to pull her back and forth. She indicated to some of the girls who walked beside her that she needed to rest. I escorted her into the office, where she sank onto the sofa. Someone brought in a flask of tea and some sweets.

Mahboba looked at us and said, 'What can I do? I can't help them all. You see. So much poverty. So many stories.'

Nazanin brought Mahboba some hand sanitiser and told her to clean her hands and face. 'What can I do? I am just one woman,' she continued as she drizzled the disinfectant onto her hands and rubbed it onto her face and palms.

Someone knocked on the door and a woman in a blue burqa came in. Nazanin asked her to leave because Mother Mahboba was resting.

'No, let her in,' Mahboba said, holding her head in her hands and resting against the wall.

'But Mother, there is a line out there already.

You'd better rest for a minute, then we will let them in,' Nazanin suggested.

'Okay. Bring me some water first. Let them line up and I'll talk to them one by one.'

As she rested I headed to the clinic, which Mahboba had launched earlier in the day. Women were lining up to get some advice. The clinic was a simple, brightly lit room with a bed, a desk, medicine cabinets and other basic supplies. A male doctor in a white jacket and a female nurse in green were attending to the long line of women and children complaining mostly of simple coughs and joint aches. They provided them with free basic medicine and detailed instructions. The women were grateful and listened with care.

A woman came in with her adult son. His right arm was missing from the elbow, where a tentacle-shaped form was hanging, like a finger. She wanted to see if there was a way to help him get an artificial limb. The doctor told her that there was not much he could do: her son required surgery. He advised her to take him to the hospital, or maybe Mother Mahboba could help him find a sponsor. The doctor said that Mother Mahboba had recently taken a boy with a disease to Australia for treatment. She should talk to her directly.

As I returned to the office, the woman and her son followed and lined up. Mahboba was now letting in the women one by one. One of the boys was attentively taking notes, which would be used to find sponsors. When I entered, Mahboba was talking to a young family with twin boys. The mother, in her early twenties at most, had her burqa pulled up. Her skin was supple, still fresh from youth, but her eyes were those of a much older woman. Both of her three-year-old sons had been diagnosed with tuberculosis. Because they had taken a long time to seek treatment, the boys' backs had grown deformed, one bending to the right and the other to the left. The doctors had said that this put pressure on their little lungs, and they would have only a few months to live. They needed to have an operation – like the one Siar had in Australia. But the family didn't have the means and there was no one in Afghanistan who could carry out this complicated procedure. Mahboba said that she would make the twins' case urgent and try to find someone who could help. But for now there was nothing she could do.

The next case was similar. A girl this time, slightly older than the twin boys, with an alarming curve to her spine. Mahboba put her case down as urgent too. With regret she repeated the same words.

I knew she really did do what she could. When we met Mahboba in 2007, Amin and I had invited her and her family to dinner. Mahboba had entered with her twelve-year-old son Soroush overshadowing a small bent-over boy, who walked with a slight limp. This was Siar.

Siar had just arrived from Afghanistan with his brother for an operation. The same age as Soroush, he barely reached Soroush's waist. His face and eyes looked as if he had aged well beyond his years. When he took off his oversized jacket, there was a huge bump on his back and chest. That was why Siar had come to Australia, Mahboba explained.

Months before, Siar had been diagnosed with tuberculosis, which had already caused severe degeneration in his bones. The doctors had estimated that if he didn't have an operation soon, he would die in less than six months. His lungs and internal organs were being slowly crushed. Mahboba had found a doctor in Australia who had offered to sponsor Siar's operation and journey. He was scheduled to have the procedure within the next few weeks, after which he was to remain with Mahboba for a year to complete his recovery.

Almost a month later, I called Mahboba to ask about Siar. She told me he had had his operation two weeks earlier. She asked whether we wanted to go and visit him, at Westmead Children's Hospital.

Siar looked like a three-year-old, lying on a huge bed with a heavy metal brace that screwed into his skull at four points. When we arrived, though he was barely able to move, he was playing a computer game. He smiled when he saw us and with great care put the keyboard away and shook our hands. We chatted, teased him and tested his English. He understood the basics of our questions, an incredible achievement given his circumstances. We were told that Siar could also sing in Hindi. With a big smile, he impressed us with his memory, as he sang a very long Hindi song.

There was a glimmer of hope in his eyes that made him look younger than when we had met him weeks before. But the process took a toll on Mahboba that I didn't understand until a few months later when I bumped into her and Soroush at the shopping centre. She spoke slowly and had dark circles around her eyes. She opened up without being asked. Yes, Siar had a good operation and he was doing very well. But it had been a huge responsibility, something she had never imagined. The operation had been very stressful because the doctor had said that there was a fifty-fifty chance of survival. His brother, who was with him, was reluctant to take the risk. It had taken two days to convince him.

After a successful recovery, Siar went home with Mahboba. With metal rods still in his head, he couldn't walk or even go to the toilet by himself. He had to use nappies. She had to wash him in the bed, spoon feed him, give him medicine, and stay up at night to take care of his needs. She felt she was neglecting her own family. This is why, on the day I met them, mother and son had left for a few hours to get Soroush some school clothes.

It wasn't until the year after that we met Siar again, this time in Kabul when he came back. He had been given a second chance at life thanks to Mahboba. His family wept with gratitude when they picked him up from the airport.

After the children with tuberculosis, the next person in the office was a beautiful woman who had brought her youngest four children, ranging from several months to four years old. I had seen her earlier in the day, sitting by herself in a corner with her children, gazing into an uncertain distance. I had taken many pictures of her haunted face and her children crawling on the muddy ground. Her husband was a drug addict and had recently been arrested, she said. This had left her with no house and no income. She slept on the street with her five children, where she had now left her eldest son to secure their spot. Because of the children, her case was one of the most urgent. But again, Mahboba could not provide any immediate support. The woman needed to give her address so they could contact her when they found her a sponsor. She had no contact details. The office attendant took her photo, and her children's. A case file was made for her and marked urgent, yet again.

I wanted to help her myself immediately, at least give her some money to set herself up. But we had spent all we had to come on this trip. I knew my father always had some money put aside for charity, so I called him. He thought something was wrong. I explained the woman's case to him. There was silence. I could hear him sniffling. 'I can help her for sure,' he said. 'Let me know where to send the money and how much.' I said I would call him later to confirm.

But she disappeared. We never learned what happened to her and her five children.

Such were the endless stories that poured in during the Widows' Big Day Out. Not only had we not found a wife for Fatemeh's brother among the women, but we were all left more helpless, desperate and exhausted.

Once Hope House had returned to an eerie silence, with just the hundred or so children who had retreated into their rooms, I found Virginia sitting by herself on the stairs near the office.

'I cannot believe my eyes. All these women. All these children. Yet no one gives a damn about them. This is what the world should see. Here we are. It is fucking unbelievable. And yet, we can't do anything. I don't know what the fuck I am even doing here.'

I sat down next to her. We had been there almost three weeks and nothing had progressed. I also didn't know what the fuck we were doing there anymore.

I felt the shadow of the despair I had lived with after we had made *Hidden Generation*. I had seen the pain of so many women, and felt there was nothing I could do about it. Then, it had pulled me into a dark place I couldn't find my way out of.

But I had to find a way now. This was why I was there.

I knew we couldn't save the world. We kept realising this the hard way, every day. But we had to find a way to keep going, even if it only helped to save one girl from a terrible marriage. Fatemeh's story had to be told. Maybe if more people heard what life was like in Afghanistan, more help would come. The women here needed somebody to give a damn.

26

When I had got out of the taxi at Istiqlal Hospital, on that hot July day in 2006, I saw that the only way to get in was through a long line of people waiting. I wasn't going to do that. I went straight to the door, which opened occasionally to let in passing cars. The doormen ignored anyone who approached. I looked through a small window in the door and called out.

Someone shouted back, 'Queue up, sister!' I told him I wanted to get a form signed, and waved it through the window. He poked his head out, took the form, looked at it, and told me to wait. Several minutes later he opened the door to let me in, and gestured for me to sit on a bench.

It was a different world inside. Sick and limbless

people sat across the grounds, huddling in the shade. Groups of women had put down rugs and were eating lunch or resting. Children swarmed, running around as if in a playground. I was startled when an exceptionally fair-skinned and balding man with a dark moustache approached and asked if I was the one who wanted permission to film. He told me to follow him to his office. We walked past the hospital garden, which despite the heat and the dust was still in bloom with surprisingly large and luscious pink and red roses.

The main entrance of the building was very dark compared to the brightness I had just left. The yellowing paint was peeling off the ceilings and the walls. It was hot and crowded with people standing around and stretchers lining up alongside the walls. The doctor led me upstairs to a corridor with fluorescent pink chairs. His room, at the end, was so light that my eyes had to adjust. Still smelling of fresh white paint, it was surrounded by large windows that let in the July sun in all its brightness. It was furnished with several sofas, covered with crisp white sheets. Around the room, on the desk, the coffee table, the filing cabinets and behind the sofas, were colourful plastic flowers which, I discovered later, were given to the sick by visitors or as a gesture of thanks. I was directed to sit on one of the sofas. An elderly man knocked on the door and brought a flask of green tea. I watched him pour tea as I explained to the doctor the intention of my visit. He sat behind his brown desk, the only coloured furniture in the room that separated him in his white jacket from the whiteness of the room.

Sipping tea, he said, 'I will give you permission. But this is a very sensitive topic. Many of the women, even if they are cases of self-burning, will not admit it. We know the truth only because they talk to each other at night and the night-shift nurses overhear their conversations.' He took another sip and continued, 'Then in the morning, they blame the faulty gases they cook with.' He paused, holding my gaze. 'Also, for some, the family might not like them to be filmed so we have to consider their consent in this process as well.'

As he signed the form, I assured him that we would be very sensitive.

Before I said goodbye, I told him we would come back the following day, but in the meantime,

I wondered if I could have permission to visit the burns unit on my way out. He picked up the phone and called one of the nurses. A young woman in a white uniform, her hair covered by a green surgical cap, walked me downstairs. Her name was Hamideh. She was incredibly calm and composed. I, on the other hand, was not prepared for what I was about to see.

The female burns unit of the Istiqlal hospital was a well-lit room that consisted of ten beds, all of which were occupied by young bandaged women. Inside, several nurses sat around a desk with a beautiful bouquet of roses that looked like it had been plucked from the garden outside. But nothing else about this room was beautiful.

The other nurses welcomed me. I took out my camera and began taking pictures as Hamideh guided me through and introduced me to the patients.

On the first bed, next to the entrance, there was a very young girl named Golafshan, bandaged completely except for her face, which was bruised deep purple and blue. Her eyes were barely open. Yellow pus was oozing around her nose from under the gauze. She was propped up to a half-seated position. Her father was trying to feed her juice through a straw. She moaned with every gulp and called out for her mother. Her father told me she was thirteen and she had been burnt when she struck a match to a gas cooker, the cylinder for which had been accidentally left open. She had gone up in flames, he said with teary eyes, her synthetic dress melting and sticking to her body in seconds, forming an inseparable second floral skin.

Across from her was a young woman who was breastfeeding a small child. She had minor burns on her body, which were covered by a blanket. I did not want to disturb her while she was nursing.

Next to Golafshan was another young girl. Her entire body was also covered with bandages, though her face had remained unscathed. Her name was Samira and she was only eleven. The nurse said that she was a case of attempted suicide but the girl had never admitted it openly. I smiled at her and took her picture.

Across from Samira was another woman who was bandaged completely, except for her face. Her eyes were closed. Yellow pus and purple medicine had seeped through the bandages on her arm and around her neck. She was in no condition to talk and was only kept alive by the IV drips and intense painkillers, the nurse told me.

Next to her was a beautiful young girl with deep brown eyes. She was bandaged around her neck and arms. Where the skin on her face showed, it was very supple and soft. I wondered if the rest of her body would ever recover to match the smooth perfection of her face. Her name was Azadeh and the nurses told me she was about fourteen. She had also been burnt in a cooking accident.

Across from Azadeh was another woman bandaged head to toe, her eyes closed. I did not bother her either.

The women in the last two beds, however, had caught my attention when I first walked in. I went up to the girl next to the window. Her mother was standing outside, behind the fly-screen, just staring into the room. This girl had incredibly hollow cheeks and empty, hopeless eyes. Her body was mostly burnt, covered in bandages under a blanket. I didn't catch her name because it was unfamiliar to me, perhaps a Pashtun name. She was seventeen. She did not say much. I didn't understand her accent so Hamideh had to translate the broken sentences she tried to utter. She had been married only for six weeks when the accident happened, Hamideh said, and she had fallen into the *tandoor*, the big oven in the ground where the Afghans cook their daily bread. There was something about her that mesmerised me. It was as though all the emotions that I had tried to bottle up on seeing these women were reaching their limit. I knew I had to be professional, so I took several shots of her, then I had to move on.

On the last bed lay a girl with Hazara features. She shared Golafshan's story but it appeared she had been luckier: at least her face had remained intact. She did not speak, only looked at me, yet through her eyes I sensed her pain and her intense need to be relieved of it. I forgot to ask her name.

I felt that without speaking she was asking me for help – it was as if she was telling me, 'You are here, you are taking my picture, do something about it.' She made me feel responsible.

I later came to understand that it was probably this silent plea that made me pursue the film and even this book, and to see them to the end.

At that moment, I wanted to hold her hand and tell her that she would be okay; that one day she could get up, run, play and go to school. I wanted to tell her that it was a beautiful hot and dusty day outside and that I could smell the cooking for lunch. I wanted to ask if she could hear the sound of the *athan* that had just started.

Instead I just sat there, next to her bed. I don't know why but this felt like the most honourable thing to do.

I eventually composed myself, bid the nurses farewell and left, taking with me the sorrow I had just swallowed, back into the sepia world outside.

Out on the street, walking along as if I had just woken up from a nightmare that wasn't quite over, I felt insecure and self-conscious. I reasoned with my insecurity. Except for my camera bag, I looked like any other Afghan university student, with a scarf and a long jacket. This made me more confident as I walked along the dust-choked road, which gradually became less crowded and turned into a semi-residential area.

The road was lined with mud houses, some of

which also doubled as shops with thick plastic windows and roughly hinged wooden doors. Odd colourful handwritten and painted signs hung above these doors: 'Ahmad Ali's Tailoring for Men and Boys', 'Bicycle Repair', 'Fresh Confectionery', 'Jameel's Barber', 'Heart of the Bride Beauty Salon'. Passing me by on the road, boys and men pushed carts selling fruit and vegetables that had wilted in the summer heat. Barefoot old men sat with their cobbling tools fixing shoes that had fallen apart.

Before I left Istiqlal Hospital, the doctor had told me that the Mental Hospital, a few blocks away, might offer potential for our film. It was where they took and kept those who had repeatedly attempted suicide or burning themselves. On my way, I looked out for it. Just as I thought I had probably missed it, I spotted it across the street, a white building with a large green door. I crossed the road.

The gate was open. I stepped in and entered a huge empty courtyard with a barren garden, an empty plot of soil where plants had been. Inside, the compound was strangely silent. An old man was sitting on a small stool in the shade, napping. There appeared to be no one else in the building. I went up to him and coughed an excuse me. He opened his eyes and looked at me with irritation. I told him I wanted to get permission to film in the hospital. 'This place is closed to the public today,' he responded. I persisted. I explained that I had been sent by the doctor from Istiqlal Hospital. He didn't care – there was no one of authority in the building at that moment. I should come back tomorrow. I said, 'We are filming tomorrow.' He opened his eyes again, looked at me and said, 'Go on. You will be the only sane person in this building, and I will follow you.' There was a glint of madness in his eyes. I walked out as fast as I could, with a rapidly beating heart.

I still wonder about the stories that lay in that building, but I didn't dare return, even the next day with Amin.

I walked a couple of blocks, to a major junction with a fruit and vegetable market. The all-male vendors protected themselves and their produce from the harsh sun with large umbrellas on their carts. Women in blue burqas dotted the male crowd. Oblivious, and still in a trance over what I had seen, I walked around for a while, hailed a cab and went back to Aina, having had a glimpse into a nightmarish world.

27

The next morning when we arrived at the hospital to start filming, the fair-skinned doctor happened to be by the door. We didn't even have to wave our letter to gain entrance. He would be right with us, he said.

Once inside, I felt like I was reliving the previous day. Nothing seemed to have changed. The sense of hopelessness and despair once again filled my being as I saw several women on benches holding their heads in their hands, and a legless man with a Pashtun hat leaning against the wall, staring into space. Like the day before, a group of women in burqas sat in a circle on the ground near the blooming garden, several of their children still playing nearby. Next to them was a woman leaning against a tree, her eyes glazed over, gazing out but not seeming to see anything.

Amin was already filming. Unlike outside, where the camera attracted a lot of attention, people in here were too sick and concerned about other things to notice us. Amin wanted me to take the second camera and film behind the scenes while we waited.

The doctor returned. He motioned to us. We followed, camera at hand. As we passed along the grungy corridor and reached the burns unit, he told us to wait while they rolled out an empty bed with dirty sheets. There were more nurses sitting around the desk. They seemed more on edge than the day before. Hamideh greeted us. Amin asked me to put down the second camera and start recording the sound for the interviews.

We started with Golafshan. Her father was still by her side, still holding a boxed drink. He looked into the camera and recounted her story. His eyes welled up as he spoke. I was more touched hearing Golafshan's story this time. The microphone was so sensitive that the slightest movement could produce a fault in the sound, so I tried to focus on making the recording. But I couldn't control myself. Tears were rolling down my cheeks. My nose started to run. I sniffed and shuffled for a tissue. I tried to hold the boom still with one hand so I could wipe my nose, but Amin glared at me. Through the earphones he could hear the slightest movement.

I blew my nose as we were moving along to eleven-year-old Samira. Hamideh asked her what had happened. She said she had been burnt when cooking. Hamideh asked her if it hurt. She moaned, 'Yes.' Had she done this to herself? 'No.' Hamideh, who knew there was a different story, asked her again. 'What happened to you?'

'I was burnt when cooking,' she insisted.

'Did you do it intentionally?'

She stared at Hamideh silently, then at us. Hamideh repeated the question. 'Did you burn yourself because you were angry, or did someone do it to you?'

After several seconds she whispered, 'I did it myself because I was afraid.'

'Why did you do it?'

Then, she began to recount her story so rapidly that we couldn't understand. Hamideh had to translate.

She had been playing with her cousin in the yard one afternoon. They had accidentally broken the newly replaced basement window. Her brother's wife was watching and scolded her, saying that her father would kill her for this. She had decided to kill herself before her father got his hands on her.

'How did she think of burning herself?' Amin asked.

Her sister-in-law always talked about it, and said the best way to free yourself from this misery would be to burn yourself.

'What was her family's response when they found out she had done this?'

'You did the right thing,' they told her.

Hearing those words, I began to cry silently. My nose was running again. One of the nurses brought out some gauze and helped me wipe my nose while I tried to focus on getting the sound right. Amin was furious, motioning me with one hand to stop.

'Do you regret having done it?' asked Amin.

'Yes, very much so because there is so much pain now.'

There was an odd silence, and we knew it was time to move on to Azadeh. She was very agitated, telling the nurses she couldn't breathe. Hamideh tried to console her but she couldn't talk. She wanted to go to the bathroom. Two other nurses came and helped her. She moaned in pain.

Then I noticed the last two beds. In the bed with the girl whose name I had not caught, an elderly woman was sitting up, observing us. The Hazara girl's bed was empty with clean sheets. I enquired after them.

The other girl had died in the middle of the night, Hamideh told me, the Hazara girl too, about half an hour before we arrived. While we were waiting outside, her body was being removed and the sheets changed.

I broke down and wept openly. I didn't care about the sound or the film. I didn't care that Amin was telling me to stop waving the boom around. I could not breathe.

Amin was insistent that we push on. After a few minutes, I composed myself as the nurses brought us some water and gave me some more gauze to wipe my nose.

With a lump in my throat and my hands shaking, I continued. Amin wanted to ask the doctor some questions. He sat down behind the nurses' desk. We wired him up.

'How can you tell which cases are self-inflicted?' we asked.

'They are easy to tell, even if they don't admit it. They are usually burned all over because they throw petrol over themselves. The accidents usually just affect one area of the body. For instance, someone who falls into a tandoor will have their legs burnt more than their face. We have come to tell the difference over the years. And as I said, they usually talk about this issue at night with the other patients. Suicide is the worst sin in Islamic culture and it is an even bigger disgrace for the family than for the woman, so usually the families and the victims do not want to admit to what has really happened.'

Another question, which we had asked numerous other people, was 'Why burning, of all the methods?'

'Because it is more accessible,' he said. 'Fire is what they use every day. Other methods are not so accessible. Pills, for example, are rare and women don't know how much to take for them to be effective. Jumping is not possible because of its highly public nature and there are few high places from where they could jump. I have seen some really severe cases of women swallowing needles and pins. One woman's X-ray revealed her stomach full of needles. She died of internal bleeding soon after being admitted. Also, the Indian culture where they burn the widow with her husband's body has influenced these women's thinking.'

'What are the chances of the women surviving self-burning?'

'Depends on the case. Anyone who has more than fifty per cent of burns has a lesser chance, not just here, but anywhere in the world. The ones who have burned less have a chance of recovery but will be disfigured because we don't have facilities for plastic reconstruction in this country.'

Amin nodded to indicate a wrap-up. Since the nurses were daily witnesses of this condition, we also wanted to interview them. Some of the nurses shyly refused, but Hamideh volunteered. Amin wanted to know more about the women's experiences.

'These women,' Hamideh said, 'suffer a lot. Those who have burned themselves and survive face an even worse return to their families. Their actions usually make them outcasts, rejects. Particularly those who are married and who burn themselves to escape their husband's family face a tougher homecoming.' She paused and lowered her voice. 'I want to tell you something. Remember that young girl, the six-week bride who died last night? She had not fallen into the tandoor accidentally. She was pushed in, either by her mother-in-law or sister-in-law, both of whom disliked her very much. She told me this the first day she came here but because her own mother was always around, and she didn't want her to know, she told everyone she had fallen in herself.'

I tried my best not to react as I listened. We would later learn that women burning other women, particularly in an extended family context, was a common phenomenon.

Amin asked Hamideh about the worst case of self-burning she had ever witnessed.

'It was a six-day bride who had married into a family where she was unwanted because they had had to pay a large dowry. From the very first night, the in-laws started scolding her, verbally and physically abusing her. On the sixth day, she poured petrol over her head and lit a match. She was brought to the hospital but she did not survive.' Although Hamideh was telling a very painful story, it seemed as though she had told it so many times she was numb to it.

We wrapped up after Hamideh's interview, said goodbye and left the burns unit. Amin was furious with me. Bad sound recording could make these interviews unusable, which was as good as not having them at all. I knew that, I told him, but I couldn't help myself.

'I have feelings too,' he said. 'Get over it for now and deal with them later.' He was partly right. My head was spinning and I was full of rage at his comment, but I decided to let it go.

As we headed out into the garden, the woman who had been leaning against the tree was now squatting by the entrance of the corridor. On the floor in front of her was a green blanket wrapped around what appeared to be a body. The body, the doctor pointed out, was that of the Hazara girl, and the woman was her mother. Hearing this, Amin unhooked the microphone and began to film her. She didn't seem to notice the camera. We crossed to the other side of the garden and watched her. She sat motionless, in silence, in a trance.

A yellow station wagon taxi backed in near the entrance. Several men got out of the car and flattened the back seats. The woman got up and wiped her face with her scarf as the men picked up the body. It seemed heavier than the young girl I had seen lying on the bed the day before. They carefully placed the body in through the boot and climbed in. Her mother followed; she sat next to her daughter's covered head and held it in her hand. All of this was done in silence. The driver shut the trunk, got in the car and slowly drove off.

As soon as the doors were closed, I heard the woman, who until then had not appeared to shed a single tear, wailing and screaming.

'My daughter, I have lost my beautiful daughter.' The car drove away, carrying the body of the young girl who at least was no longer in pain.

Still in shock, Amin filmed the car as it drove off.

Suddenly I felt very hot. I was about to faint. Amin complained, asking why was I just standing there instead of taking pictures. I snapped that I was still holding the microphone. He didn't need it any more.

I did not feel like taking pictures. I was feeling sick, I told him.

'How can you feel sick now? We have work to do, pull yourself together.'

I wanted to throw my bag on the ground and start screaming. Instead, I took a deep breath and headed towards a boy selling cold drinks out of an icebox. I had not realised I was so thirsty. I gulped down the sweet nectar, which instantly made me less dizzy. I sat down on a bench next to some women. Amin had nearly finished packing up his equipment. Everything was in slow motion, as if we were immersed in water, and our limbs could only respond so fast.

Just as we were walking out of the main gate, another station wagon taxi identical to the one we had seen leave, drove in. I waited to let it pass, casually glancing inside. From the corner of my eye, for only a second, I saw the red face of a woman lying across the back seat, just as the body of the Hazara girl had been placed in the other car. It took me some seconds before I realised what I had seen. I shouted to Amin. He turned back and took out his camera to capture in awe the scene we had just witnessed, in reverse.

A woman wrapped in floral sheets was being pulled from the back of the taxi. Her bare shoulders, raw and scorched. Her red face, chapped and peeling, her lips bloated and bleeding. Doctors and nurses ran to the car. They placed her on a gurney. She moaned loudly as they transferred her to the bed and rolled her into a room next to the entrance. The doctor signalled us in.

I was unable to focus but I had to record the sound correctly. I steadied my shaking hands by leaning them against my body as I held the microphone. In contrast to our sense of urgency and shock, the doctor, the nurses and the other attendants were all very calm.

An elderly couple accompanied the burnt woman. As the doctor questioned the parents, he set out to examine the extent of the burns. He tried to lift the sheet from her body but she moaned with the smallest movement. The sheets had become inseparable from her skin.

'What happened, sister?' the doctor asked as the nurses started to clean her.

'She fell into the tandoor,' the mother replied.

'When?' he asked, examining her hands.

'About twelve days ago.'

The doctor repeated in shock, 'Twelve days ago? Why didn't you bring her in earlier?'

The father responded, 'We didn't have any money.' The mother corrected, 'Her husband didn't let us.'

Conscious of the camera, the doctor tried to lift up the sheet again to show the extent of the burns, but the woman screeched in pain. He looked at her legs, which were scorched even more badly than her shoulders. The doctor said there was definitely severe infection. 'We must pull off the sheets, clean her and bandage her,' he observed.

'How old is she?' he asked the parents.

'Twenty-six, and she has a child.' She was just a bit older than me.

The doctor looked at the red-faced woman on the bed, unravelled in anguish. 'Don't worry,' he said, 'we will fix you up and you will be well, like a fresh flower, in a couple of weeks and can go back to your child. Okay? Don't worry. It will not hurt.'

He told us that they needed to pull off the sheets but they had to do it next door. He didn't think it would be appropriate for Amin to be there. I was welcome to come in. I declined. I had seen enough.

We left the room and waited. Amin was anxiously filming with no obvious purpose. I sat down and tried to breathe deeply. Now that I was seated, my body was shaking.

Some time later, I don't know how long, when I had stopped shaking and was breathing normally, they rolled her out. Amin turned his camera towards the woman and followed as the attendants wheeled her across the garden. I ran after Amin with the boom mic. The bed was rolled into the burns unit, and all the way to the end where the Hazara girl had been. The woman groaned as they transferred her to the bed. Amin went close to talk to her but she didn't seem to hear us, nor the nurses who were asking her questions to keep her conscious.

They had to sedate her. They injected something into her arm and told us that we had to leave, now. We quickly got out of their way. We went to the garden and sat there for some time. I was shaking again.

No one came to tell us we could come in again. Once we could get up, we decided to leave.

That night in the shower, I wept for those women. I wept until the tears were spent. But the next day, there were more.

The next evening we called the doctor to see what happened to the woman. He said she had died earlier that afternoon. I felt myself being swallowed by a ball of sorrow. On that day I realised that sorrow, like happiness, freedom and love, could be infinite. I had felt it in every shaking cell of my body. As a human being, and most of all as a woman, I was also left with an immeasurable sense of responsibility.

Part III

28

Nik Mohammad skipped and hopped through the light drizzle, came into the office and sat next to Mahboba on the edge of one of the springless sofas. He had been avoiding Mahboba, but with time running out she was determined to meet him, so after the Widows' Big Day Out she had invited him to Hope House for a cup of tea.

Seddiq sat behind his desk at the other end of the room. Nik Mohammad was a slim man with white hair and weathered skin. His narrow eyes darted around sharply and nervously, as if waiting to detect a trick or prove a point. He wore a white Afghan *shalwar kameez*, and on his right shoulder hung a clean green and white chequered shawl.

As he walked in, Mahboba introduced us as filmmakers from Iran. At first he was opposed to the camera, glancing around to find out what the truth was. But Mahboba told him that the film would greatly contribute to making people understand life in Afghanistan and he agreed to the entire wedding being filmed. From that moment onwards we and our camera became invisible to him.

Mahboba ssaid how nice it was to see him. She had missed him. She wished him and his children well. She asked him how he was doing and why he would not think about his own life. 'Why don't you find a nice wife for yourself? She will take care of your children.'

He stared at her sharply. 'Are you kidding me? I can't do that, sister. She will want me to take her to parks, to entertain her. I can't do that.'

'No, we'll find you a nice woman who will sit at home and take care of your children.'

He flung his hands in the air and tapped his temple with his right hand. 'Come, sister, you are hurting my head with this nonsense. My head hurts even thinking about it.'

'Listen to me, this is good for you. Help yourself.

You have sat around like a crazy old man. A nice woman will help. I will find you a nice woman.'

'Sister, it is past me. Stop it. My head really hurts thinking about it. Let's sort out these kids first. I will go along with whatever plans you have made so far. I will go anywhere you want me to go, I will do anything you want me to do…'

'My plan is to get the wedding under way as soon as possible before I leave.'

'Well. Okay. But that's beside the point. They will get married anyway. I am talking about long-term plans, six months from now,' he said.

'We will find your son a good wife, and she can take care of your children. We have been looking but haven't found anyone yet. Give us three months so that we can find a suitable person. Someone good for your children.'

He stared at Mahboba. 'Then give me some money in the meantime so that I can have something to offer in return for a nice girl. I will leave the money with Fatemeh and Abdul Fattah until we find someone.'

A long pause. Abdul Fattah sneaked into the room and sat in a chair at a distance from Nik Mohammad.

'But I don't have any money. I don't have the means

to pay you anything. How much are you asking for?' Mahboba replied calmly but firmly.

'I already told Ostad Seddiq.'

'That's a lot of money.'

'Okay. I'm willing to negotiate. That's no problem. I'm stuck, that's why I say these things. It's not like I want to get rid of my daughter. She hasn't finished school yet.'

'You see, what you are asking for is almost ten thousand Australian dollars. I don't have that much money. Let's do this: I can pay you a smaller amount now, then I can send you a bit more later, little by little.'

'No... I can't do that. It will be hard on me. I don't have time.'

'You are not giving us two months? Time for what? What do you want to do? Where are you going?'

'It will ruin me. I can't do that. Please judge for yourself. I am in a bad position,' he said, his eyes gleaming.

'I understand where you are coming from. I know you are a good person, and your intentions are good. Let's do it this way, then... You first said you would split the costs. I will spend half for the wedding, you put in the rest,' Mahboba said.

'No need for that. I will pay for that. I'll bring a nice lamb. We'll roast it, invite twenty people and have a small wedding.'

Seddiq, who until then had been observing this exchange in silence, taking occasional deep breaths, rubbing his temples, suddenly interrupted. 'Listen,' he said louder than both Mahboba and Nik Mohammad, 'when you came to me a while ago, you said you wanted to get your daughter married. She was the first priority.'

Nik Mohammad turned around and stared intensely at him, his eyes slanted and accusing. 'Yes, I came to you and I said why don't you marry her to your son.'

'My son doesn't want to marry her. He's young.'

'Listen, then you came to me and said you'd find a wife for my son instead,' Nik Mohammad said, still staring at Seddiq with accusing eyes.

'Yes,' Seddiq said.

Nik Mohammad leaned forward and then the men began to speak over the top of each other.

Mahboba tried to intervene. 'You speak to me, brother. Forget Seddiq. You are dealing with me...'

They ignored her and continued to argue over each other, louder and louder. Abdul Fattah got up and left the room.

When there was a moment of silence, Seddiq said, 'You insult us with what you say. Learn how to speak, then come and talk to women… You are making fun of us, it seems.'

'No, you are making fun of me,' he came back.

Mahboba loudly intervened. 'Listen, Seddiq. Nik Mohammad here is like my brother.' Then she turned to Nik Mohammad. 'I understand what you mean. I know you love your daughter. I know you are mourning for your wife and you are alone. I understand you…'

'But…'

'Listen to me.'

'I…'

'Listen to me.'

'But…'

Mahboba cut him off, 'Stay calm. I understand you want to solve your problems. I want to help you. If no one understands you, I do.'

'God bless you. May you live long…'

'Listen to me! I promise I will not ruin your

household. Just give me some time to find a nice woman for your son.'

'Just pay me something now. Abdul Fattah is also my son. I will leave the money with them, then we will look for a nice girl ourselves.' Pointing his finger at Seddiq, he continued, 'Seddiq here gets mad at me if I say it. He has brought me pictures of ten or twelve girls. But we couldn't go to see even one of them. What am I to do?'

Seddiq replied and the men got into another loud argument. It went on until Seddiq got up and left the room.

We watched him leave in silence. Mahboba said, 'Listen, Nik Mohammad. Let me pay you a smaller amount. What you ask is ten thousand Australian dollars. I don't have that kind of money now. I will go back to Australia and beg and bring it back to you. Just let this wedding happen. Instead you will have Abdul Fattah. He is a wonderful boy. He is honest. His heart beats for your daughter...'

'I understand that...'

'You know every day there are people who come here and ask me to give, give, give. I am just one woman. Governments don't pay me. I don't have so much to give. You have to understand me too…'

'I understand that… Okay.' He wrapped his shawl around his shoulder and pulled up his socks, ready to leave. 'You said you had another girl to show me. Let's go see her.'

Abdul Fattah, who had sneaked into the room again and was sitting at the back, looking solemn, said that the girl lived nearby. 'We can go see her together.'

'There is a picture of her. Abdul Fattah, why don't you show us her picture?' Mahboba suggested.

Abdul Fattah left the room and promptly came back with a digital camera. Flipping through the images, he found a picture of a young girl of about fifteen. Nik Mohammad looked at the camera at arm's length. 'Okay. Let's go see her first, then I'll talk to you later about it.' With that, he left.

Mahboba sat back in her chair, exhausted, and smiled at the camera. We seemed to have a story.

29

The search for a wife for Fatemeh's brother had reached across Afghanistan through Mahboba's network. Even though everyone had a suggestion, nothing had gelled. The people in and around Hope House were especially keen to help; they sensed the pressure building up as Mahboba's departure drew closer.

Among those who made a particular effort was Setareh, a young girl who travelled a long distance every day to learn sewing at Hope House, and to hang out. I had seen her around. She was about fifteen or sixteen, plump, loud, and coarse. She always chewed a huge piece of gum far too big for her mouth, which she moved around with her tongue when she spoke. I liked the way she defied the traditional norms of how a teenage Afghan girl should look and behave.

Mahboba had asked Setareh whether she wanted to marry Fatemeh's brother, and she was one of the first to be introduced to Nik Mohammad. Just at the mention of her name, he had rejected her without a second thought. She said he had narrowed his eyes and stared at her, and said, 'Are you kidding me? I don't want a husband for my son.' Setareh was not one bit distraught by his rejection. 'Who wants to marry him anyway? I am happy,' she said when she heard his reaction. 'I know so many girls my age who need to be married to be saved from their own families. I'm okay.'

She did seem to have an endless supply of cousins, neighbours and acquaintances with daughters of marriageable age. She introduced so many girls that we nicknamed her The Agent. Among them, though, only two agreed to a meeting.

We set out to meet the first girl on a hazy afternoon. We had no clue where she lived. Setareh volunteered to direct us. Virginia, Amin and I, along with Mahboba and a few of the teachers, piled into the van with the broken windscreen and left ourselves at the mercy of Setareh. Following her instructions we drove across Kabul and turned into a mountainous suburb. In the labyrinth of dirt alleys, with each basic straw and mud-brick house indistinguishable from the next, it seemed that she was lost. As we kept driving – left here, right there, in the maze of streets, with a tinge of uncertainty in Setareh's voice – Mahboba became impatient. Did she know where she was taking us? Yes, she assured us with a nod and a chew on her gum.

We drove down narrow potholed paths that had turned into small lakes from the previous night's rain. Jameel constantly had to swerve around children playing in the puddles, trying to keep the van from either skidding and hitting a child, or getting stuck in the mud. Before either of these happened, to our relief, we reached a dead end. Setareh told us to stop. She suggested it was not a good idea for Amin to come in. Mahboba agreed. The families in these areas were traditional and would not like to have an unknown man enter their house, especially to hear talk about such a delicate and private matter as their daughter's wedding, and particularly not a man with a camera. I didn't have much to contribute inside, so I stayed with Amin while Virginia went with Mahboba.

Even though we could not have a camera inside, Amin wanted to at least record the sound. We knew that perhaps if we asked for permission for the sound to be recorded, it could have jeopardised the entire situation. And yet, this was a crucial step in the film we were trying to make. We might have ended up not even using the recording, but at that point we made a choice. Amin decided, against our ethical conscience, to record the sound without telling the family we were doing so. He wired Mahboba with a powerful radio microphone which she clipped under her scarf, and hid the reception device inside her clothes under her armpit.

After they had entered the house, Amin and I left the van. Curious children gathered around. Amin began to film in the street, but a few adults were watching us with suspicion. Jameel, observing from a small corner store where he was smoking nonchalantly, came up and whispered to Amin that he should stop filming.

'People in this area are not that open,' he said very quietly. 'They might just shoot us if they don't like that we are filming their family members.'

Setareh, who was also waiting with us, agreed.

She suggested we go up to the roof of one of the neighbours, from where we could see the house where Mahboba had gone. Amin could already hear Mahboba, as she settled into the room and started a conversation with the family. Setareh guided us up a set of rough cement steps, through a neighbour's yard, and into someone's house. We ended up on a roof. Amin set up his tripod and began to film. Setareh pointed to a backyard next door, indicating where Mahboba was.

Just then, a young girl wearing a purple and white Afghan dress walked onto the balcony, where she stood as if to get some fresh air. Setareh whispered excitedly, 'That's her. That's my cousin, the girl they are proposing to!'

Amin filmed the girl for a few seconds, until she noticed us and ran back inside. My heart started beating faster at this – things could go wrong really quickly. Setareh gave a squeal of jubilation but Jameel picked up on my unease. 'Pack up please, I don't think it is a good idea,' he whispered urgently to Amin. We quickly took our gear, walked back down the stairs, and put the camera away in the van. We waited, casually playing word games with some of the children until everyone else returned.

We piled into the van and headed back to Hope House.

'So, what happened?' asked Virginia. Although she had been inside, she had no idea what had been said.

'Basically, they are asking for too much money,' Mahboba replied. 'And the woman is not even her real mother, she is her stepmother.'

Virginia thought the woman seemed mean.

'Well...yes, she saw the situation and thought she could use us because we are desperate. And that poor girl. They have pulled her out of school.'

'To do what?' Virginia asked Mahboba.

'I don't know. She doesn't leave the house. It is like they are imprisoning her. But I don't know why,' Mahboba said.

'So they didn't agree?'

'No, but they didn't disagree either. She said she needs to talk to her husband. He will call Seddiq. But I think they are asking for too much money.'

'So, not only do you have to pay for a wedding, you have to pay the dowry too?' Virginia said.

Mahboba let out a strange laugh. 'Yeah, it seems

like that.'

'Oh, my goodness. How are you going to do this, Mahboba?'

'I don't know. We will just wait and see what happens – if they call Seddiq or not.'

A few days later the father did call Seddiq, asking for the equivalent of ten thousand Australian dollars, and not settling for anything else. Seddiq told him thank you very much, but we're not interested, and that was the end of that.

In the meantime, Setareh had introduced us to another girl. Abdul Fattah had given her a small digital camera to take pictures of any girls with potential. It was one of these pictures that had been shown to Nik Mohammad when he met Mahboba at Hope House, and he had shown an interest in the girl.

Mahboba wanted to make plans to meet her. But on the same rainy day that Seddiq got the call from the other family, the girl herself came to visit Hope House with Setareh. She was dark-skinned, with large eyes and a slight lisp. She was wearing a grey long-sleeved Afghan dress with matching pants and a shawl. Seeing them come in, Amin and I picked up our equipment and followed the interaction between Mahboba and the girls. There was a moment of confusion. She seemed unsure when talking to Mahboba. Mahboba got the impression that the girl didn't know why she was there and snapped at Setareh, 'Are you kidding us? Every day you bring a new girl and waste our time? Does this girl even want to get married?'

'Yes, she does.' Setareh giggled. 'I already spoke to her mother.'

'We don't have much time. I cannot let you play around with us like this,' she warned.

The bewildered girl, who had been watching this conversation silently, interrupted, 'Of course I know what I am doing. I think there was a misunderstanding.'

'Okay, as long as we are clear.' Mahboba turned to her, 'God willing you will be the right match. Fatemeh's brother is a good boy with a good income. You will be happy with him. You will have a roof over your head and warm food to eat.'

There were giggles between the girls. Mahboba said, 'You know he has little brothers. Can you take care of them?'

The girl, suddenly serious, turned to Mahboba and said, 'When you marry someone, you marry their whole family and they become your own. If they need care, you take care of them.' She had already accepted this role and this destiny.

'You are so wise. I think Nik Mohammad should meet you today. But look at you, you look like the entire weight of the world is on your shoulders,' Mahboba said.

The girl laughed as she put her hand across her mouth.

'Have you spoken to your mother already?'

'Yes, she knows I am here and I am meeting you.'

'Okay, then we will come and see you and your mother today. But first we need to clean you up. No one will want to see a girl that looks like this. Come, Sanaz and I will fix you up.'

We went upstairs to Mahboba's room where she kept her suitcase. Amin handed the camera to me as we went into the room. Mahboba had nothing for the girl to wear, so she decided to give her one of her own dresses.

I began to clean her up, starting with her feet.

They looked as if she had dipped them in mud and let them dry. I gave her some wipes and she scrubbed her toes.

Mahboba went through her suitcase. She tossed a few things around and pulled out a brand new Afghan dress of maroon and dark green, with matching pants and a shawl. 'You change into this.'

With clean feet, the girl shyly stripped down, covering her exposed chest, and quickly put on the new dress.

I put the camera on the tripod. Mahboba gave me her own make-up case. I wiped down her face, put on some light foundation, and drew a very thin line around her eyes. I followed this with a dab of blush and subtle lipstick. Her already large eyes looked even bigger and brighter. She looked at herself in the mirror, smiled and put her hand over her mouth.

Mahboba gave Setareh some money and instructed them to take a taxi home and wait for us. 'Don't change anything,' she said. 'We will be there in a few hours with Nik Mohammad.'

Nik Mohammad turned up at Hope House with his youngest son. The boy, no more than seven, had terrible deep marks on his forehead and near his eyes, said to be caused by a poisonous salak, a centipede whose bite and tail leave deep scar tissue. If not treated immediately these can last a lifetime.

Abdul Fattah appeared too, showered and dressed in new jeans, an ironed shirt, and a freshly shined pair of dress shoes. It was beginning to drizzle, so we quickly squeezed into the van. Pari and Virginia stayed behind.

We drove for a good while on the main road, then turned into a muddy side street. The van climbed up through the mountainous suburbs of mud brick houses, and down across an isolated valley which was beginning to fill up slightly with water. From here, we went up another mountain and reached a large plateau. There was nothing in this vast empty space except for a few houses dotting the landscape at a fair distance from one another. We passed several makeshift homes built coarsely from stones, with plastic sheets as windows, and some tents. Jameel was counting the houses. Setareh had given him directions.

We had been on the road for more than half an hour. The rain was picking up and the plateau was becoming a river of mud. The wheels of the van whizzed. Mahboba was afraid we would get stuck, so she instructed Jameel not to go any further. He stopped about a hundred metres from our destination.

There was nothing and no one around on this flat land. As far as I could see in the rain, there was only one more house, some distance away. I understood now why the girl had had such dirty feet when she arrived at Hope House, and felt terrible for my judgement. There was no sign of any cars. She had walked all the way through the mountains, the valley and the mud.

We trotted to the house. Like the others, this was a simple cubic structure made of stones and mud, emerging organically from the earth. Its thick plastic windows flapped violently in the rain and wind, which by now had picked up considerably. Nearby was a well with a hand-press pump from which the family drew water.

A young woman in a black dress and matching shawl, holding onto a young child, came out to greet us. She guided us inside, where we took off our muddy shoes. She pulled up the thick curtain that covered the doorway.

Waiting inside to greet us was the girl – unrecognisable. Her face was covered with white powder. Where I had drawn a subtle line around her eyes, there was glittery purple and pink eye shadow. Her lips were painted bright red beyond their normal size; her cheeks were bright pink.

Mahboba, who was right behind me, exclaimed loudly and turned pale. 'What have you done to yourself?' she whispered under her breath before Nik Mohammad could enter. She tried to stall him by walking slowly as she signalled the girl to go and wash her face. But he pushed in to seek shelter from the rain before she had a chance to get away. One glance and he did a double take. He scratched his head, his eyes darting left and right, looking for an escape route. But he had no choice. Mahboba quickly pushed him into the next room, where the mother was guiding us. He took the shawl from his shoulder and wiped his forehead, suddenly beaded with sweat as he took the five steps from the entrance to the living room. The young woman introduced herself as the girl's stepmother and welcomed us, oblivious to what had just happened, while we tried to overcome our shock.

The room was cold and damp. The floor felt wet under my feet. The walls were unpainted and coarse. Large cushions were placed around the walls to create a barrier against the leakage.

Nik Mohammad folded his knees and awkwardly sat on them, ready to spring up and leave at the first opportunity. The stepmother sat comfortably near the door, across from him. Mahboba was glancing from Nik Mohammad, who seemed more ill-at-ease every minute, to the stepmother, Amin and me.

The stepmother, who had noticed the discomfort, thinking that it was the house we were taken back by, broke the silence, 'This is our humble house. This is all we have.'

Nik Mohammad wiped his forehead again. His eyes shifted uncomfortably around the room. 'Okay. That's good,' he said wiping his forehead with his shawl.

'I think he did not like your daughter because of her make-up,' Mahboba said.

'No... The thing is...um...no...people...' Nik Mohammad, lost for words, wiped his face again. 'Maybe my son...maybe he can decide for himself.'

'Where is her father?' Mahboba asked.

'He works from very early to really late at night,' the stepmother replied.

'Oh, okay,' said Mahboba.

There was another silence.

Then Mahboba asked how many children the woman had, and how old they were. After a few short answers, the conversation died.

'Maybe we can have a cup of tea,' suggested the stepmother.

'No,' responded Nik Mohammad, and he started to get up, half squatting, then very slowly straightening up, while everyone else was still fully seated and looking at him. 'We should go because…the other children…they will come from school… There is no one…to…um…open the door for them.'

Mahboba glanced around the room and then at Amin, behind the camera.

'Let's have some tea?' Amin suggested too.

'No, no…' Nik Mohammad said, and unfolded his knees fully, his eyes darting around at everyone until he was standing up. We were all forced to follow him.

Mahboba let everyone else walk out first. I stayed behind with her. Setareh suddenly turned up from the other room. She, too, had a white face, pink cheeks and red lips. She was chewing a bigger piece of gum than usual.

'Why did you do this?' Mahboba asked angrily. 'Why did you touch her make-up? I told you not to touch anything.'

By now the girl had come out and was standing in the shadows. She had wiped her face clean.

'I didn't do it. Her stepmother did,' Setareh said.

I had no idea how many people lived in the house, but a number of young girls were lurking in the hallway entrance.

'Everything is ruined,' Mahboba whispered to no one in particular. Then out of desperation, she asked the stepmother if she was willing to marry her other daughters.

'Yes,' she said, 'as long as they are taken care of.'

She told the girls to come out with her. Nik Mohammad was almost halfway to the van, already soaked and sinking into the mud with every step.

Mahboba shouted, 'Nik Mohammad, come have a look at their other girls.' The girls were following.

'Sister, I am not interested. Let's go. The boy will be home and there is no one to open the door for him,' he said, not turning around.

'She has beautiful eyes.' Mahboba was almost running after him through the mud, dragging one of the young girls by her arm.

He turned back towards her, grabbed her by the sleeve and guided her to the van. 'Sister, please. They are too young. I am not interested. Let's go.'

'At least look at them. You are being very rude.'

He didn't even bother to respond. The family had all come out, some five or six girls huddled together in the rain, watching this awkward moment unravel.

Abdul Fattah's freshly shined shoes were now brown with mud.

We piled in. Jameel started the van. It would not budge. The wheels turned but we didn't move.

The girls still stood in a cluster, watching as the van sank deeper into the earth each time the wheels turned. Several minutes passed like this. Nothing. Amin suggested that we were not moving because the van was too heavy.

'Let's get out then,' agreed Mahboba.

We stood together nearby as Jameel tried again. Nothing. The family continued to watch. The wheels churned mud. Jameel suggested they call a taxi to get us home first. Mahboba and I were instructed to sit in the van and wait. As we sat, the girl tapped on the window through the rain.

'I wanted to give you back the dress.' She handed a plastic bag to Mahboba.

'No, no, keep it, please. It is yours. I am sorry it did not work out,' she said, gently pushing the clothes back into the girl's hand.

'No, I am sorry. I don't know what I was thinking.'

'Please don't be disheartened. You are a beautiful girl. You have a great future. And if ever you want to come down to Hope House, I am looking for help for the children. I want someone to be there in the morning to help the little ones when they wake up. To go to their bedroom, caress them, brush their hair and teeth, dress them and put cream on their hands. Just come down any time when you are free and tell the head teacher that I told you to come.'

Abdul Fattah knocked on the window. 'No taxis will come here. They know they will get stuck now. We are going to try one more time to clear the van. If not, we will call for a truck. Please get out. I am sorry, but we need the van to be lighter.'

We stood in the rain in what was fast turning

into a giant swamp. Without moving, my feet were sinking into the ground. As Mahboba and I held hands, Jameel brought a couple of shovels from the house and the men began to clear around the wheels. But the more they dug, the further the wheels sank. Then everyone, including Amin, who set his camera up on the tripod, pushed while Jameel put the van in gear. Forward and then reverse. Nothing.

Abdul Fattah's brand-new jeans were ankle-deep in mud. His shirt was splattered with back slush from the turning wheels.

The sun was sinking behind the mountains. We had been there for over an hour when Nik Mohammad turned to us and said, 'I have to go now. My son, he will be coming soon and will be stuck behind closed doors.' With that, he piggybacked his smaller son and set off through the mud. He had a good three to four kilometre walk ahead of him across the plateau, down the valley and across the village before he could reach any public transport. We watched as he disappeared in the rain.

Jameel was unable to organise a truck that would come in less than two or three hours. It was getting dark and cold. Abdul Fattah and Jameel were on their phones to discuss options with people at Hope House. One suggestion was that if we walked across the valley and up the mountain, taxis might consider coming there.

Abdul Fattah volunteered to walk across first and keep in touch. I watched him slush through the mud and disappear. Mahboba held my hand and we stood very close to each other, our feet sinking in the mud. Amin continued filming, as if unaffected by the situation. We waited and watched as Jameel tried again to clear the wheels one last time. The van sank even deeper.

We started to walk. Hanging on firmly to each other, Mahboba and I left Jameel by the van and started walking through the swamp towards the valley. Amin had rolled his pants up, put on his Pashtun hat, and was following us, camera in hand. This was gold for the film and he knew it. Every step became heavier than the last. We walked like this for a while, making slow progress. Mahboba, who was wearing a long skirt and sandals, kept one hand on my arm and with the other held up her skirt. Then, with one step Mahboba's foot came up bare. Her sandal was sucked deep into the mud. Setareh, who was following us closely, ran to dig up the shoe.

Mahboba threw her jacket on the ground and let go of my hand. She kicked off her other sandal and began to walk ankle-deep in slush, wiping tears from her face. I glanced at Amin. He ran to her, still filming, and said, 'Mahboba Jan, I asked for drama and God gave it to me.'

'See, Amin Jan. Let's hope we don't die for this film!' she replied, half-serious. She kept walking, Amin next to her, I behind, and the two girls running after us with the sandals in their hands. 'I am so angry and sad. All of this. And nothing. I have to give up my life for this? And those sandals. I bought them in Dubai. The only nice thing I bought for myself. The only thing I had left all to myself. Even that is ruined. I have had it.'

Amin made gentle fun of this woman who until now had seemed unbreakable. 'Your Dubai sandals. So special. That's okay, you can get another pair.' Mahboba turned to him, crying and laughing at the same time. She looked at me and we both chuckled at the absurdity.

The girls had by now caught up with us. They had brought a jug of water and washed Mahboba's feet and the sandals. One by one, they put the shoes on her feet. The Dubai sandals would become the joke of the trip.

After this comic relief, Amin, Mahboba and I continued walking along the almost liquid landscape, hand in hand. Setareh and one of the girls from the house, who walked this path daily, accompanied us to make sure we were on the right track. Until now, it had all been flat but ahead of us was a slope down. Mahboba and I descended slowly, deliberately sinking our feet deep into the slush so we wouldn't roll down. We were almost at the bottom when Amin fell headlong, camera at hand, almost knocking us over like dominos. He quickly recovered, now head to toe in mud. He had held his camera aloft so that not a drop of mud lay on it. Mahboba and I burst out laughing.

'You could have broken your neck,' Mahboba said.

'But I saved my camera,' he said proudly, wiping the lens with the inside of his shawl.

Back on flat ground, we continued. Setareh and the girl followed at a distance. There was nothing in sight except the flatness of the land ahead, until we reached another downward slope. This was the valley we had crossed in the van on our way up. It was now a raging brown river. We slowly climbed down and stood in disbelief. It was a river of debris, carrying all sorts of refuse from the villages above, a tennis shoe, paper, clothes, rags, food scraps and, at one point, a syringe.

Two schoolgirls on the other side braved their way across. One skipped over a few rocks, slipped and fell right in, her schoolbag soaked. The other ran to help her and fell in too. Now wet, they just walked the rest of the way across thigh-deep in water.

As we stood thinking of strategies, Abdul Fattah appeared on the other side. He had somehow managed to bypass the valley without getting wet. When he saw us, he removed his shoes and socks, rolled up what was left of his new pants and walked across, knee-deep in water. 'I will help you, Mother Mahboba, don't worry,' he said.

Abdul Fattah was preparing Mahboba to cross over when Amin pounced and skipped across on a couple of stones, ready to film as Abdul Fattah assisted Mahboba. Mahboba took off her Dubai sandals and held them in her hand. She pulled up her long flowing skirt, exposing the thick, dark leggings underneath, and held Abdul Fattah's hand. Together, they cautiously crossed the surging river of rubbish. Once they were safely across, Mahboba jumped up and down with joy.

I was still stuck on the other side. Amin handed the camera to Abdul Fattah, who continued filming. He was already wet too; he walked through the water towards me, put me on his back and carried me. Everyone clapped.

Setareh and her friend bid us farewell from the other side. Mahboba's phone rang. She stood silently listening for a while. When she hung up, she threw her arms up in the air and hugged Abdul Fattah. 'It was your father-in-law. He said he is sorry and did not want to cause us so much trouble. He has seen how hard we are trying to find a wife for his son. He has agreed to let the wedding happen, if we pay him the money only. He doesn't want us to find a wife for his son. He is willing to negotiate.'

This was a curtailed happiness, a moment of defeat and victory. He had not agreed to the wedding unconditionally. He still wanted payment, but somehow it was a relief. Mahboba still had no means of paying him but she was glad because she knew finding money in less than a week would be easier than finding a wife for a boy we had not met.

By the time we reached Hope House, it was pitch black and we were encrusted in mud. When I stepped out of the taxi my shoes were invisible under lumps of mud that had hardened into clay. Later, I took off my jeans and threw them straight in the bin. There was no way the mud was coming off without some girl scrubbing them for hours in cold water. I longed for a hot shower where I could stay under running water, and let the day and the memory of the mud wash away. I wiped my body down with wet wipes instead and got into bed.

We had just over a week left in Kabul.

30

The next day we did get to wash the mud off. Jameel drove Mahboba, Pari and me to a small muddy side street, next to a rusting hand-painted sign: 'Women's Baths'.

Mahboba didn't want to reveal to the women in the baths that she was hosting foreign guests. Before we got in she instructed us: I was to be the daughter-in-law who had returned from Iran, and Pari was to be a distant mute cousin. We laughed at our parts, thinking we could pull it off.

In anticipation of a much-needed wash, I tried to overlook some unpleasant details. The entrance to the bathhouse was covered with a thick grey plastic curtain that when moved smelled like a wet rag that had been left in a corner and had never dried. Inside was a dingy chamber lit with a few large yellow outdoor lights that could withstand the intense moisture. The ceiling was low and dripped occasionally with decades-old condensation.

A middle-aged woman with her hair loosely tied back reigned over this bathhouse, sitting on a chair behind a high table – so high that we had to lift our faces up to see her. Her skin was dull and her face not welcoming. It was as though she had been there so long that she had moulded onto the wall behind her. Mahboba reached up as high as she could and paid her.

I was instructed to take off my shoes and put them in a plastic bag. Pari silently followed. As others stripped their blue burqas and hung them on the hooks on the grey tiled wall that dripped with moisture, we took off our loose scarves and jackets, which we carried with us to the next room. There was another curtain that may have smelled even worse than the first, but by now my senses had adjusted. In this dark room we peeled off all our layers, putting everything into plastic bags. We only took with us our toiletries, and headed to the next chamber, which was separated by a thick piece of plastic.

Unlike everyone else, who was stripped bare, Pari and I kept on our underwear. This gave us away. I was wearing pink cotton boylegs, the colour and cut immediately giving away a foreign-bought object. And Pari revealed a small tattoo on the back of her shoulder, which showed she was not a mute cousin from just around the corner after all. Mahboba had not expected this.

The other women stared. Mahboba quickly guided us past the plastic curtain and into the final room. It was cleaner than I expected. With high ceilings and bright fluorescent lights, this was a steam room in the middle of which was a large slab of marble. Naked women were lazing around this altar piece, rubbing their skin with various homemade cleansers, scrubs and shampoos. I observed how comfortable the women were in this space. This inner sanctuary, hidden behind so many layers of chambers and curtains, was probably the only place where they could be fully at ease with their own bodies, where there was no shame, self-consciousness or fear about the display and care of the naked female form in all its beauty.

Mahboba instructed us to sit. The women began

to talk to Mahboba and naturally asked about us. Our story was beginning to fly. Or at least I liked to think it was.

Mahboba washed us gently as if we were her children. She took a giant red bucket and went to the end of the room where, from behind a short wall, she brought some hot water. She sat Pari down, put hot water on her head, shampooed her hair, scrubbed her body with a loofah she had bought especially for us, and rinsed her. Then she did the same for me.

When we retraced our steps back out I didn't feel any interest in the curtains, the mould or the ancient droplets of water. I was too clean and felt too loved by Mahboba to care.

31

Mahboba had scheduled that day to follow up on a number of other projects. The first was to find a site to set up permaculture. She believed that many of the problems of the widows and orphans could be solved if they had a self-sustaining way to grow their own food. She envisioned buying a large plot of land and bringing experts from Australia to train the locals, with the hope of creating a source of sustenance and income.

That morning, Mahboba had made an appointment with someone who was going to help her do that. This man, whose name I didn't learn, was wealthy. He had recently transformed barren land near Hope House into one of Kabul's most immaculately groomed parks. This garden, for which he charged a relatively expensive entrance fee by Afghan standards, had become one of Kabul's popular destinations for upper-class families who could afford to head to the foothills on the weekends to escape the dust-choked city. At the same time, the park was a source of income for many families in the area who were hired to maintain it. The man behind the park knew Mahboba well. It was he who had helped her buy the land on which Hope House was built. He often invited the Hope House children to come and enjoy the park for free.

Mahboba was to meet him for breakfast. And of course we tagged along. When we arrived, showered and clean, the staff greeted us politely and guided us to the balcony of a restaurant on the second floor, overlooking the oasis. The park had large green patches of well-kept grass where day-trippers could set up their picnic rugs. Systematically planted young saplings would one day provide shade. The scent of the many pink and white roses, for the first time in the whole trip, reminded me that it was spring.

Two tables had been set up for us. Covered with pristine white cloths clipped into place, like at an expensive restaurant, they meticulously displayed rare food in Afghanistan, including toast, soft rolls, a platter of various cheeses, and tiny tubs of imported butter and jam. The waiters brought pots of green and black tea, and jugs of juice. We glanced at each other. This would have been considered basic, just average, anywhere else. But for Afghanistan, at that time, this was five-star dining.

The big boss came and greeted us in well-spoken English, and told us to enjoy our breakfast. Then he sat down and started a conversation with Mahboba at the other table. Half an hour later, it was concluded that he was unfortunately unable to donate any land, given his current financial situation. This park had taken a lot from him and it was still struggling. However, he would be happy to help Mahboba look for a plot of land that could support the project.

He would uphold his promise. I found out later that he helped Mahboba's Promise buy some acres of land, which Mahboba eventually transformed into a permaculture project.

As part of this initiative, they also turned the empty patch of land inside Hope House into a useful garden which produces apples, pomegranates and easy-to-grow vegetables to help feed the children. When we returned to Hope House and were discussing the wedding, a well-known British painter came to give art classes. He was an artist in the Queen's court and had come to Afghanistan on a mission. His mission, though, as we later learned, was manifold. He had been brought to our attention by the man who had promised and failed to raise funds for our trip. He had been put directly in touch with Mahboba's Promise and they had arranged for him to teach some classes while we were there, with the possibility of painting a mural in Hope House. We had actually met the artist during our first week in Kabul.

On that afternoon we were in Mahboba's office where we were filming her encounter with a middle-aged-looking young woman and her seven- or eight-year-old son, who was weathered like an old man, with black, calloused hands. She was a widow whose husband had been killed as a bystander in a fight between the Taliban and the Americans. She had two younger daughters in addition to the son she had come with. With his father's sudden death, the boy had become the family's breadwinner overnight.

She said, with a shaking voice, that she wished her other children were boys too so that at least they could bring in some money. To support his family, her young son shined shoes on the street. This was a futile task, redundant really on the muddy or dusty streets of Kabul. She wanted her son to escape this misery. As his mother spoke, the boy broke down. 'All I want is to go to school,' he said through sobs. 'I don't want to shine shoes for the rest of my life.'

Mahboba began to cry too. She pulled the boy towards herself. 'I promise you, I dedicate my life to you and all the children like you so that you can all be educated and live a good life.' But there was nothing else she could do at that moment. He had to wait for a sponsor.

It was in the middle of this conversation that the British artist had arrived. He had been silently let into the room where we were filming. Someone had whispered translations of the conversation to him and he had then immediately left the room. As the boy and his mother were leaving – he in his once beige shirt which was now almost black and she in a torn blue burqa – this man stood in the corridor, his hair perfectly combed to the side, wearing a white shirt, tweed jacket, khaki pants and shiny shoes as if he had just been airlifted to this place without touching the ground in Kabul. He stepped aside as the mother and child left, and then came into the office.

I thought he had left the room so as not to disturb the filming. But when the family had gone and we were being introduced to him, he quickly said that he did not want to be part of this film or any project we were doing, because, he said, we were making a political film.

Mahboba was surprised. Why did he think we were making a political film?

'You are talking about the Taliban and the Americans. This is a political film. I don't want to be part of it. I was not under the impression that you were making a political film,' he reiterated.

There was an awkward silence. Virginia, who had been with us, tried to explain to him that the boy and his mother were simply recounting the events that had affected them. They were in no way making any political statements. But he was insistent, and there was nothing we could do to convince him so we let the matter rest.

Over dinner, as we sat on the floor in the room

upstairs, eating a simple meal of beans and bread with our hands, the artist revealed his grander intentions. As a court artist, he was devoted to perfecting his skills. He wanted to find the rarest bristle to paint some intricate details of a portrait. On this trip he planned to travel on horseback to sketch and paint across Afghanistan, and reach a remote region where a specific breed of horse was raised. He wanted to take strands of that horse's tail to make a special brush.

We were as flabbergasted as we were amused. Mahboba asked me in Farsi to make sure she had understood correctly. When I repeated the conversation in translation, she said, 'Aaah...okay,' and gave me one of the meaningful looks that she always did in awkward situations. Seddiq, too, had a conspicuous smile on his face, as he ate in silence, trying to cover up his reaction.

Mahboba changed the topic. When could he come and teach the children? He agreed to come back in a few days to chat with Mahboba and Abdul Fattah about how he thought they should run the class.

He had returned on the same day that we went

to the mountains to propose to Setareh's cousin. He arrived mid-conversation again, this time one between Virginia, Mahboba and Seddiq as they stood around the yard at Hope House. We greeted him as his car drove in, and he disembarked, as clean as before, and joined us. Virginia told him that we had just come back from proposing to a fourteen-year-old who was locked up in a house.

He responded, 'Surely that is wrong on so many different levels. It is paedophilia to begin with.'

Virginia chuckled and said, 'Look around you. Then everyone here is a paedophile of some sort. Come on. This is Afghanistan. But the question is how do you stop this? These poor, poor children.'

'I am sure the authorities would be able to do something about these cases. This is surely against the law, the selling and buying of underage girls.'

Mahboba and Seddiq looked on, amused.

'But it is so much more complicated than this,' Virginia said. 'And I am only beginning to understand it.'

'Surely they can do something about this?' he insisted.

'Yeah, but, what? I mean, people here don't even

know how old they are. People's births are not even registered properly,' Virginia said.

Mahboba jumped in. 'Yes, for example, I don't know if I am fifty or fifty-two. My mother tells me I was born in the winter. But my older cousin tells me it was not the case. No one knows.' She laughed. 'I could be forty-five, fifty or fifty-something. I believe I am thirty-five.'

Oblivious to Mahboba's comment, which had us giggling, the artist persevered earnestly. 'So there you go, that's the way to solve the problem. The government should start getting everyone registered, creating birth certificates for people so that they know how old people are.'

Whether he was joking or not, we couldn't tell. But his comment was so uninformed of the actual situation of Afghanistan, so off-hand, that we didn't know whether we should laugh or respond seriously with a multitude of reasons as to why this was not a priority for a country struggling with abject poverty, corruption and war.

Seddiq laughed it off, slapped him on the back, and told him we should go in for a cup of tea, and so the absurd conversation ended.

This time he had come back to Hope House to actually teach the children art. We headed to the class where twenty or so boys were sitting behind their desks, eager to learn from this master painter. He was waiting outside the classroom, groomed to perfection again to the point of obnoxiousness, in a crisp white collared shirt and beige pants. Together with Amin, with his Pashtun hat, two-week beard, and trousers he had unrolled for the meeting in the park, he went in. We were to document this, but he asked us not to use it for our actual film. It was for documentation only. I followed, microphone in hand.

Rahman, one of the English teachers, had been nominated to interpret. The children, clearly intimidated, stopped playing and sat up attentively, and he began.

'Hello, everyone.' He gave his name and said he was from England. The children stared in silence. 'I grew up, like yourselves, not very rich.' He paused for the translation. Rahman gave a rough interpretation.

'But I worked very hard. I loved art. I painted and sketched day and night as a child the same age as you.' A pause, followed by another even rougher translation. The children started to shuffle in their seats.

'Because I worked hard, I got a scholarship to go to the best art school in Florence. There I studied fine arts under the supervision of some of the great masters of our time, including…' He named a few people. This time the translation was made up. Rahman skipped the part about Florence, possibly because neither he nor the children knew what or where it was.

Then he wrapped up his speech. 'So I want to tell you that you, too, if you want, can one day become a good artist. You just need to practise.'

Translation: 'You can be successful.'

'Let us begin by learning how to draw, then. Okay?' He looked at Rahman, who nodded and told the children to say yes.

He then drew a circle on the chalkboard and began talking about perspective. He held a pencil to demonstrate the scaling of an object, position and distance of the facial features in relation to each other. He looked at one of the boys, drew a quick circle and sketched in eyes that very much resembled his.

Rahman gave up translating. He just told the children to copy what the artist was drawing on the board. 'Draw a circle and then eyes,' he said. They followed the instruction.

For forty minutes he sketched, explaining complicated concepts of distance between eyes and nose, and shadows. The bored boys kept kicking each other under the table to keep entertained and produced stick figures by the end.

'And that is the end of the class today,' he finished. The children ran away as fast as they could. He stood at the door overseeing them go, radiating with self-satisfaction. The children had learned nothing.

Later, he got himself just a slight bit dusty as he kicked some football with the boys, who were playing barefoot on the cement court. After the obligatory game with the orphan boys, which he made sure was captured with photos, he put on his tweed jacket, this time chequered green and blue, got into the clean car waiting for him and left. Mahboba saw no point in inviting him back to do a mural.

32

Mahboba had even more plans for that afternoon, the most important of which was to negotiate with Nik Mohammad. Now that there was an agreement to pay instead of finding a wife for his son, Mahboba needed to convince him that he was asking for far too much money. This was a crucial time, and although Nik Mohammad had no objection to us or our camera, we didn't want to take the risk of upsetting him by intruding into his house at that point. But this conversation was important for the film. Amin wanted to record it. So that evening, near dusk, Amin wired up Mahboba with the radio microphone. We went up to the roof to film her walking across the valley into Nik Mohammad's house. Abdul Fattah followed us, and put on the headphones to hear the conversation.

By then, we hadn't yet seen Fatemeh. Even Abdul Fattah had not seen her in weeks. Nik Mohammad had locked her in the house. Mahboba greeted the family, paying special attention to Fatemeh. She scolded Nik Mohammad for keeping her prisoner. She said she felt dishonoured by him, that after all that she had done for him and his family, he didn't even trust her enough to send his daughter to school. He mumbled vaguely in response.

Mahboba began to talk to him about the wedding. She reminded him how much trouble he had caused everyone in the previous weeks. He apologised. He just wanted to make sure his children were settled. Mahboba started to negotiate with him. At first he resisted. Then she said that she would take charge of the wedding and pay for everything. He didn't need to spend anything. After the wedding, his daughter could still live at home with him. Abdul Fattah and Fatemeh could live in his spare room.

Abdul Fattah went pale as he heard this through the headphones. His eyes first narrowed and then welled up with tears. He turned away from Amin.

'I was not expecting this. I had never thought of living with them.'

In the background, while Abdul Fattah drifted off, Mahboba managed to convince Nik Mohammad to let the wedding happen on the coming Saturday. It was also decided that the couple would move in with him, which meant that the household would not lose Fatemeh. He agreed.

Then Mahboba persuaded him to lower the dowry. 'I cannot afford the amount you are asking. Let us negotiate a reasonable price. And as I said, I will pay for the wedding.'

'My dear sister,' he said, 'in a few months, I have to go and find my son a wife. I need to use that money to be able to approach a decent family. Please understand my situation too. I have no source of income. My son has very little and Abdul Fattah also makes next to nothing. Think about our well-being too.'

'I have thought about your well-being. Your children are all being educated at the school. They eat breakfast, lunch and dinner at Hope House. When she is older, she can start work there and gain experience. Money is not all that matters. There is a young boy out there whose heart is beating for your daughter. Can't you understand that?'

'I understand that. But how is that going to help me?'

'See, you don't understand. Why don't you find a wife for yourself instead of bothering these kids? Maybe then your head will work properly.'

'Please. Sister. Stop this nonsense. Not again. Let's focus on the children.'

'Okay, so I want to offer for your daughter to be a bride in the next week. We will buy her nice clothes, throw a party, and they can get married this Saturday,' Mahboba said conclusively.

It was Wednesday night.

'Okay. I understand that…'

'You don't understand,' Mahboba interrupted. 'I can give you five thousand Australian dollars. That is all I can afford. Even that I don't have. I have to borrow it, and then go back to Australia and beg to be able to pay it back here. Have a think about what I am saying.'

'You are shaming me now. You make me sound like I only care about the money. I don't. I just want to ensure my children have a good future.'

'Okay, then I guarantee a good future for your daughter. It is settled. Later, we can even help you find a wife for your son.'

There was silence.

'You put me to shame,' Nik Mohammad said quietly, almost to himself. 'I have no choice but to agree.'

'Congratulations, my lovely Fatemeh. Let us go now and start the celebrations. You are so fortunate,' Mahboba said.

Abdul Fattah dropped the headphones and ran down the stairs.

Mahboba said her goodbyes and headed out. Amin and I followed Abdul Fattah to greet Mahboba at the Hope House door. When she arrived at the gates, Abdul Fattah ran and kissed her on the hand. She hugged him and jumped up and down. 'We did it. We have a wedding to plan!'

And so it was that we finally had a wedding happening. In three days.

Mahboba decided to stay at Hope House that night to talk to Seddiq and Abdul Fattah about the wedding plans. We returned to the cousin's house and slept happily in our warm bed.

33

The next morning Mahboba welcomed us with dark circles under her eyes. She had not slept. Discussions about the wedding had gone well into the night. A decision was made to hold a henna ceremony on Friday night, and the wedding on Saturday. When Mahboba was about to go to bed, she was approached by some of the local women who had found out she was staying there for the night. They had been waiting in the grounds of Hope House to see her. Into the night they whispered the horrific stories of their lives into her ears. After the women left, some of the girls and boys turned up. They wanted Mahboba to tell them happy stories. The older ones left at some point, but the younger ones had fallen asleep in her bed. Then, very early in the morning, someone woke her to take an emergency call. A woman from UNICEF wanted to know, urgently, if a boy could be brought to Hope House. They wanted to meet with Mahboba, in private, as soon as possible. Half-asleep, she had divided the wedding plans and responsibilities between Abdul Fattah, Seddiq and some of the older girls before the women from UNICEF arrived.

Mahboba told us about the case after the women from UNICEF left. Late the night before, somewhere in Kabul, the police had picked up a nine-year-old boy with detonators around his body. He was about to be blown up on a suicide mission but the controls had failed. He had screamed for help and the police had picked him up.

In some remote villages, extremely poor parents sometimes sell their children to religious groups. In Islamic law, a boy reaches adulthood at fourteen, so no boy younger than that can be prosecuted or held responsible for a crime. If caught, the child is usually returned to the family, but this puts the family at risk because the child has the potential to expose the plot and identity of the people responsible. Often, the group will eradicate the entire family.

The police did not feel it safe to return the boy to his family immediately, and they had contacted UNICEF for his safekeeping. UNICEF does not have facilities to take care of children. Instead, it works with other organisations that have the means to do so, such as Mahboba's Promise. There was, however, further complication. The boy appeared to have been sexually abused. This meant he required an additional type of care to see him through the physical and psychological trauma.

Mahboba was due to get back to UNICEF as to whether Hope House was in a position to look after the boy. I watched her make the call. Her eyes were brimming as she said they could not take him. It was too dangerous. He could be traced to Hope House and jeopardise the entire centre. Mahboba also tried to reject cases of sexually abused children because the centre did not have the right psychological care for them.

Unfortunately, cases like this one were common, especially at that time with the 2009 presidential election just around the corner. One of Mahboba's cousins, who worked for the police, had told her that in just a few days they had caught at least fifteen potential suicide bombers, many as young as the boy she had turned down, some even younger. The groups behind these attacks usually targeted crowded areas or governmental offices, strapped the child with explosives, and blew them up remotely.

A few days earlier, we had been potentially in direct danger of exactly this kind of attack. Virginia had been in contact with the ABC office in Australia. Once she felt safe enough to stay for the entire duration of her planned trip, she had proposed to do a short story on Mahboba for the ABC's *7.30 Report*. Part of the plan was for Amin to film a thirty-second piece of Virginia talking directly to the camera on a busy Kabul street.

We decided to do the filming on our way from the cousin's house to Hope House early one morning. We hooked Virginia up with the radio microphone and Bashir stopped the van in the middle of a crowded market. Life was going on as usual all around us. Men with carts were selling fruit, SIM card sellers were stalking potential customers, and women were busy haggling and buying household essentials as they waved away children pushing them to pick up all sorts of useless goods.

As soon as Virginia stepped out of the van, the crowd noticed her. In the male-dominated market, dotted with only a few blue burqas, Virginia stood out in her green scarf and white top. In seconds, hundreds of people swarmed around her. Some were saying things to her. Others wanted to sell her stuff. Small children latched on, begging for money. Virginia panicked. Jameel shouted out loudly but the crowd didn't disperse. When this proved useless, he physically formed a one-man barrier, pushing people back with his arms wide open.

After five tries, with many interruptions and unwanted comments in the background, Virginia managed to get the thirty-second piece done. It took us ten minutes. By that point, both Jameel and Mahboba told us to wrap up even if we were not done.

We didn't understand at the time that if we had stayed longer, we would have made ourselves a target, giving attackers time to strike.

Mahboba raised her fears with us only after telling the UNICEF office she could not look after the child. We didn't know until then the extent of the unseen safety precautions and security we had around us.

At the taekwondo competition, for instance, she had made sure that the club's doors were locked from the inside. She had also set someone to monitor the movement in the hall. No strangers were allowed inside. When Amin and I had stayed at the half-built house, unknown to us, some of the older boys had slept behind our door, while two others had stood guard all night on the roof. Even when moving around, she said, in case we didn't notice, we always either left early in the morning or after dark. 'I told you you would be safe,' she said to Virginia after she had revealed all of her hidden security strategies.

We now had to start planning the wedding in earnest. It was Thursday morning. We had to organise a henna ceremony for the following day, and a wedding in two days.

We started with the shopping. Afghan couples begin their life together by purchasing essential personal and household items. What they deem essential varies, of course, depending on their means.

Abdul Fattah and Fatemeh's needs were the barest basics. While other couples might spend weeks and even months making purchases, for them, with their wedding planned only two days in advance, that afternoon was all they had.

Nik Mohammad hadn't let Fatemeh out of the house in weeks, and he agreed to do so now under one condition: he was to accompany us at all times. Seddiq took this as a sign of Nik Mohammad's continuing mistrust. But there was nothing he could do, as Nik Mohammad and his younger boy crammed into the van along with Abdul Fattah, Fatemeh, Seddiq, Pari, Amin, Nazanin, two other teachers and me, to go shopping.

The first time we saw Fatemeh, she was waiting to board the van with us. She was wearing a long pink dress topped with a tan jacket, and a long scarf that covered half her dark brown braided hair, which reached almost to her hips.

There was an unease in how she carried herself. She held her head down, her gaze glued to the ground, and she did not look anyone directly in the eye. She held her arms across her chest, with her back rounded slightly. We greeted her warmly, having looked forward to this moment since we had arrived. She momentarily looked up, nodded without any changes in her facial expression and continued to look at the ground. I could tell the pressure that Nik Mohammad had put on her had generated a lot of tension in her. She had no idea of our anticipation to meet her, or the effort that had gone into making her wedding happen.

In the van, Fatemeh sat next to the window. Nik Mohammad seated himself between the couple. During the drive, I was watching the interactions. Abdul Fattah cautiously eyed Fatemeh on several occasions to see how she was doing. She kept staring out of the window, not even once turning around to look at us or Abdul Fattah. When Abdul Fattah and Nazanin wrote a list of things needed, Fatemeh seemed uninterested. It was as if she wasn't even part of the plan.

Jameel stopped the van in a side street near the crowded central bazaar by the river. Thousands swarmed around the marketplace on this muddy day. Beggars, shoppers, sellers, and children selling gum, plastic bags or matches crowded this wide street.

Handicapped old men sat on top of their carts, among the oranges, bananas and vegetables, shouting to attract the attention of burqa-clad women. The smell of burnt oil from deep-fried vegetables rose from food stalls; the homeless children stared hungrily. Bicycle bells rang to open up the way, while a legless boy rolling around in the mud wearing a pair of shoes on his hands laboured to get himself out of their path. Shopkeepers lured in shoppers by asking if they were looking for anything special. Pedlars competed with the shops, displaying assorted cheap goods from ladies' underwear to shampoo, razors, batteries and plasticware. Butchers hung whole freshly slaughtered lambs from their stalls as they cleaned out the carcasses, entrails and blood spilling on the ground, the stench overpowering a nearby business where an old man was selling assorted homemade fragrances in awkwardly-shaped bottles.

It was an overwhelming place, and walking through it all was a young girl, out of the house for the first time in weeks, with the bottom of her pink dress dragging in the mud, blood, and excrement on the ground, with her friend tightly holding her hand and her father, her young brother and her soon-to-be husband confidently walking behind them. Amin and I followed, filming their every move. Jameel and Seddiq walked behind us, deflecting unwanted attention.

Once we were inside the plaza, the madness lessened. Here there was nothing but fabric. Hundreds of shops, protected from the rain, beggars, sellers and chiming bicycles, sold identical-looking material. Shop after shop, roll after roll: everyone sold the same cheap, sparkly and colourful imported fabric. Seddiq and Abdul Fattah picked a shop, as good any other, and stepped in.

The store was covered wall to wall, floor to ceiling, with rolls of cloth. The shopkeeper immediately recognised us as a bridal party. He greeted us, selected a few different kinds of material and rolled them out on the large tables for Fatemeh to choose. The selection included inelegant, coarse laces of bright pink, green and purple with varying patterns. As Abdul Fattah, Nazanin and one of the teachers were picking patterns and colours with interest, Fatemeh stood in the middle of the store, unengaged, looking up at the ceiling and around the store, holding one arm across her chest. When everyone settled on a heavily patterned green lace and asked Fatemeh if she liked it, all she did was nod her head without even looking at what was picked.

I saw her react the same way in the shoe shop, where Nazanin and Abdul Fattah chose several pink, gold and green glittery sandals. She kicked off her own muddy footwear and tried on the elegant shoes for size and nodded her head. Again in the store where they bought a suitcase. 'Do you like the green one or the blue one?' Abdul Fattah asked. She looked around but did not respond, as if she had not heard him. When the girls picked out underwear for her, again she stood there, staring at all the Chinese-made bras hanging around the walls.

As we walked back through the crowd, Abdul Fattah carrying a large suitcase over his head, Fatemeh holding on to some bright pink buckets, her father walking behind them, plastic bags in one hand, dragging his youngest son along, I observed Fatemeh's behaviour. I realised it was not a lack of interest. This was probably the first time in her life that this teenager had come so far into the city and into the crowded marketplace. It was not shyness and indifference: she was overwhelmed by all the colours, sounds, smells, and people, and more importantly by choices. She just didn't know how to carry herself and how to respond.

We piled into the van, barely fitting with all the shopping, and headed to the Sewing Centre where the ladies were waiting to measure Fatemeh and make her dress.

Seddiq and Amin then headed back to town so that Seddiq could borrow the dowry money from a local lender. I stayed behind to film the jubilation at Hope House.

When Seddiq returned later that afternoon Mahboba walked across the small valley without hesitation, knocked on Nik Mohammad's door and gave him the money. She had no idea how she was going to repay it. But with that, she saved Fatemeh's future.

34

We had been in Kabul for almost a month and Mahboba was running out of time to attend to all of her projects. Negotiating the marriage had taken a lot out of her time. The day of the henna ceremony was the only window left to visit the Panjshir Valley to tend some of the projects she ran there.

Mahboba was from the Panjshir Valley, so she was excited to take us to her home. While I had heard about its majestic beauty from her, nothing could have prepared me for the wonder we encountered. About a hundred and fifty kilometres north of Kabul, the valley sits at the edge of the Hindu Kush mountains and is bisected by the Panjshir River. Home to some 140,000 people today, it was the site of the Panjshir offensive during the Soviet war, and more recently fighting between the Taliban and the Northern Alliance under the command of Ahmad Shah Massoud, a national hero born and raised in this region.

Our drive from Kabul to the valley took us through small villages, open farmland and barren lands where tank shells lay discarded, a reminder of the war's constant presence in the background of Afghan lives. Along the way a structure hundreds of metres long glimmered against the horizon, almost like a mirage. This was the infamous Bagram airfield and prison. Run by the Americans, it was one of Afghanistan's most notorious prisons, mostly housing political prisoners, with a long history of torture. Past this, a winding, narrow road ran into a deep valley and along a river, surrounded on both sides by snow-capped mountains.

As we drove into the valley, we were told it was full of myths and stories. Panjshir means 'Five Lions'. According to legend, five brothers protected the valley in the eleventh century. Because of their bravery, the people saw them as lions, and the area was named after them.

Before the gated entrance to the valley stood a small shack made of rough mud bricks. An elderly man with a long white beard, dressed in an old army uniform, was diligently scrutinising every passing car. This man, Mahboba told us, had been living in that house for the last thirty years, since his son died fighting. He had dedicated his life to protecting the valley in the small way that he could, standing guard day and night to make sure no major harm could reach it.

At the gated and guarded entrance, anyone who entered or left the valley was identified and their details noted. Mahboba was familiar with this process. Virginia, however, was uncomfortable. She had been, after all, strictly advised by the Australian Department of Foreign Affairs not to travel outside of Kabul under any circumstances. She hid her face by looking out of the window.

'Hello, brother,' the guard, armed with a rifle, greeted Jameel. 'Welcome. How can we help you?'

'We have Sister Mahboba Rawi here, of the Rawi family. She is the founder of the school in Abdara and we are going to visit the school and her family.'

Mahboba lowered her window. 'Hello, brother. I

think I know you. Are you not the son of ——? He is my cousin.'

'Yes, sister, I am. Good to see you. Of course. Welcome home.'

'Thank you, brother. I have some guests that I want to take into the valley so they can see this beautiful area.'

'Of course. I need to see some identity cards for them. Who do you have?'

Jameel pointed to Virginia in the back. 'We have one foreign guest.'

'What about the rest?' the guard asked, looking at Amin, Pari and me.

'The three are locals, our Iranian sister and brother, and our Pakistani sister,' he said, pointing at each of us.

Amin, Mahboba and I silently chuckled at Jameel's remark.

'Oh, okay. Iran and Pakistan. Can I get an identity card for the foreign lady, please?'

Mahboba translated. 'They need to see some ID from you.'

'Only from me? But I don't have anything on me,' Virginia said nervously.

‘She did not bring her passport,’ Mahboba told the guard.

‘Okay no problem,’ he said. ‘Brother, could you please fill out a few forms then for us?’ He motioned to Jameel, who quickly jumped out of the van.

We sat waiting in silence. Virginia began fidgeting with the corner of her scarf. She kept wrapping it around her finger, twisting it and then letting it go, again and again the entire time Jameel was talking to the guards. He returned laughing with the other guards. Virginia stopped twisting her scarf.

‘Have a safe trip. Welcome home, sister.’ And the gate was opened.

At this point, the landscape changed. The valley became wider. To our left, on the bank of the vigorously flowing river, were some rusted Russian tanks.

‘These tanks have been here for at least twenty years,’ Mahboba said. ‘I remember, when we were young, the river would wash down all sorts of things. Once, after a big fight with the Russians, we watched many bloated bodies floating down.’

We reached a point where there was nowhere to go but down towards a narrow bridge across the river.

'This bridge,' Mahboba said, 'was not here. When we were children, we couldn't cross here. No cars could. We had built a small bridge from some wood that only carried people. It meant we didn't have any cars in the area. But when a big rain came or the river was overflowing, we were stuck on one side.'

Across the river, we were at the foothills of another range of mountains, surrounded by orchards blossoming to their fullest on this early spring day. The grass here was literally greener than on the other side, or any side I had ever seen. The sky was much bluer, and the clouds were like fairy floss, drifting slowly between mountains.

This was a hidden paradise, utterly different from the bustle, noise, mud and dust of Kabul. Women were picking crops in the fields. In the distance, sheep were grazing on flat lands. And there was no sign of the usual heartbreak of begging children. Instead, healthy children were playing in the field, chasing each other like butterflies.

Mahboba had several projects to check on in Panjshir. The most important that day was to visit the school. Here, there were only two schools: one was for boys, built by an American organisation, and the other, built by Mahboba, was the first ever in the area dedicated to girls. This school was built on a slope, overlooking the mountains and the orchards. Since its opening several years earlier, more than three hundred girls had been educated here every year.

As we drove to the bottom of the slope, girls in clean uniforms of blue overalls and white scarves were already lined up on the stairs to greet Mother Mahboba and her guests. This visit was important for several reasons. A great part of the activities that happened here was supported by School's Promise, an initiative of Mahboba's Promise that builds ongoing relationships between well-off educational bodies in Australia and schools in Afghanistan. The Abdara Girls' School was a sister school to Asquith Girls' High School in Sydney.

Students from Panjshir regularly communicated with their Australian sisters through letters, photos and little crafts, like friendship bracelets and embroideries. These activities raised awareness and built cultural connection between the two countries. More importantly, they raised funds, an essential element in this relationship, paying for teachers, buses and classroom furniture. When we arrived, the girls had painted large banners displaying their gratitude: 'Thank you our Sisters at Asquith Girls' High School'.

Our entourage was greeted with clapping and cheers from the children on the stairs. Then we were directed into a hall where nearly three hundred girls were seated on the floor, taking off our shoes in the sea of footwear at the entrance.

Because back then technology was hard to access in these remote areas, Mahboba's Promise often struggled to show sponsors in Australia proof of where their support was going. We had been instructed to record and document as much as we could on this trip and to make our footage and photos available to the office.

As we got into the hall, I sat in a corner from where I could see the girls and take photos without interrupting or being noticed. At the front of the room were stacks of booklets, pencils and pens. Mahboba said a few words, then the female school principal invited students up by class and handed out packets of stationery. I observed the girls as I took their pictures. They were well-behaved and respectful during the ceremony. Once the formal part was over, the girls relaxed and chatted. Mahboba encouraged the older girls to do exceptionally well so that they could be hired as teachers at the school once they had finished their own studies.

One of Mahboba's cousins, who had just graduated from high school and had started sewing basic dresses for her neighbours, was in Panjshir. Mahboba wanted her young cousin to introduce a tailoring course to the school. The older girls huddled around her to see what was on offer as she cut a simple pattern from a piece of newspaper, showing how that could be transferred and used to make part of a pair of pants. The girls oohed and aahed at the possibilities.

I started moving around the room to capture these wonderful moments on camera. Here, the people had a different appearance, unique to the region. Most of the girls had fair skin, large brown eyes, and some almost blonde hair. The morning light shone through the hall and the girls made striking models. As I basked in the beauty of these girls I reflected on the impact of Mahboba's work. If it were not for her work, none of these girls would have had the chance to be educated and their lives would have looked very different.

Of the hundreds of portraits I took, one captured the essence of what I felt that day. It was of a first-grader with a red scarf tightly wrapped around her head, her lively eyes filled with awe. There was a sense of uncertainty, a melancholy and yet a strange happiness in her gaze.

Next on the Panjshir agenda was the livestock project. With support from Australia, Mahboba's Promise lends rural widows a calf and a cow for eighteen months, as a source of income, running an accompanying simple course on cattle management. The women targeted for this project are poor widows, with little or no education. We were going to meet the first participant. To reach her, we walked through the blooming orchards and the lush green land along the river. The air was fresh, fragrant with cherry blossoms.

Our destination was a coarsely made two-storey mud house. A stooped elderly woman greeted us from an upstairs window. Frail and barely able to walk, she limped out a few minutes later and gave

Mahboba a warm hug. Her skin was marked with deep lines, and the hair showing from under her black scarf was hennaed bright orange. She gave us a big toothless welcoming smile. She was probably no more than sixty but she looked as ancient as the mountains surrounding the valley.

She wobbled ahead and ushered us in. We soon learned that the cow had become a central part of her life. The entire ground floor of her house had been transformed into a barn. The cow lived in a dark room on the left. To keep it warm, the woman had boarded up the window, letting in only a small opening of light. Hay was stacked in another dark room. As Amin filmed and I photographed, she made Mahboba peer into the dark room. Nothing was visible. Mahboba suggested that she should bring the cow out into the open later so we could take pictures for the office records.

The woman led us through the barn and up a few dark stairs into her living quarters. It had walls of rough mud, against which she rested cushions and large blue and aqua blankets. There was a small lopsided dish cabinet to one side, standing with one leg balanced on a rock. But the main feature of this room was the windows which wrapped around and opened right into the tops of the blossoming trees. One could reach out, touch the leaves and talk to the birds from here.

We sat down and a young girl dressed in purple shyly brought us a flask of green tea, some cups and a few plates of assorted nuts and raisins. The walnuts, the raisins and the almonds were juicy and sweet. Mahboba told me that everything here was a local product. One of the reasons that the Panjshir Valley had remained so secluded, and had managed to survive through the turmoil, was its self-sufficiency. The trees around us produced fruits like walnuts, apricots, mulberries and apples. In the summer, the villagers ate the fresh fruit and nuts, and in the autumn they dried them for winter. Those who kept cattle produced some of the best dairy and meat in Afghanistan. Most did not have refrigeration, so they cured the meat and hung it to dry in the cooler seasons.

Mahboba wanted to take pictures of the cow before we left. We waited under the shade of the trees as the woman limped out with her son next to her, holding onto a loose rope tied around the neck of a scrawny cow. Mahboba looked at me and then at Amin with a half-awkward smile.

'This cow...it is too skinny. What did you do with it? Don't you feed it?' she asked.

'Yes, we do,' the son said, 'but it was sick for a while.'

Mahboba turned to us and said in English, 'How are we going to show this one? It is almost dying. Try to get it on an angle that makes it look like it has some meat on its bones at least.'

Virginia and I giggled as we took pictures of Mahboba with the frail lady who could barely stand and a skinny cow next to a tree. As we were about to wrap up, someone ran in with a banner, which they attached to two trees with a rope. They had spelled livestock as 'livestack'. Now we had pictures of an elderly woman with a toothless smile, a misspelled banner, a scrawny cow and Mahboba next to a tree. But even this was to be appreciated by the Australian office, which hardly ever saw images of sponsored projects.

The mesmerising beauty of Panjshir Valley was luring us to stay and spend all afternoon among the orchards, or even to stay longer and get to know the people and history of this exceptional place, but we had to go. The peacefulness of the valley we had just left behind stayed with me as we headed back into the frenzy of Kabul and straight into the henna ceremony.

35

We reached Hope House just before sunset. Everyone was waiting for us, so the henna ceremony could begin.

I had seen young girls spending their afternoons putting henna on each other's hands, fingernails and feet, squeezing the thick brown paste from a cone like icing on a cake. Historically, this brown paste was considered to represent sensuality and good fortune, which is why a henna ceremony is an auspicious tradition to begin the festivities for a wedding.

Hope House was vibrant and brimming with excitement. I went to see what the girls were up to. A few had gathered in Arezoo and Maryam's room. On top of the donated red Qantas bedcover lay two broken plastic-handled mirrors, next to palettes of shattered glittery eye shadow in bright pink, yellow, green and blue, and blunt lidless pencils of various colours. One of the girls brought a small make-up bag and emptied out the contents of lipsticks with broken lids, dried-out mascaras, and more pencils, some so small they could hardly be held, and various shades of nail polish. Next to this, they had combined all their colourful, jingly plastic jewellery. The girls were rummaging and pulling out whatever they felt would match their outfits.

I began filming. Arezoo and Maryam put bright eye shadow on each other's eyelids, on occasion stopping and posing for me playfully. Other girls joined in. When Arezoo and Maryam had finished with their faces, they brushed each other's hair. Arezoo went to her green metal cabinet and brought out a dented rusty tea-tin full of small pieces of paper rolled to different lengths, and a ball of elastic bands. Someone brought a glass of water and a bag of little twigs with elastic attachments. The girls dampened and curled each other's hair with the bits of paper, or the twigs, and tied them over with elastic. Not long after, they turned up outside with their curled hair, shimmery eye shadows, and in their better clothes.

They played carefully in the yard waiting for the party to progress.

Not in the same way as the girls, we also needed to compose ourselves before joining the festivities. Mahboba went to her room to rest and freshen up. Pari, Virginia, Amin and I waited in the office and cleaned our equipment. I asked one of the girls about Fatemeh and was told she was getting ready. Did I want to go to see her?

I took a film camera and headed to the house across the valley. Nik Mohammad did not mind the camera. We were very familiar with this house as we had filmed it from the Hope House, but this was the first time our camera had gained access inside.

Nik Mohammad's house was simple. Beyond the high brick walls there was a small unkempt garden with twiggy trees and small saplings that were barely standing. In the centre of the garden was the well and a hand pump from which the family got their water. A cement path led to the house. The house was divided into two parts by a small alcove where shoes were taken off. I was directed to the right, to a room that was painted rose pink. Hope House was clearly visible from a small barred window. This was where Fatemeh would perch all day waiting to get a glimpse of Abdul Fattah.

As I walked in, Fatemeh was sitting on the floor leaning on the cushions against the wall. A few girls were helping her get ready. She looked up, and for the first time she smiled and greeted me properly. I felt a connection with her. I held back my tears behind the camera.

Fatemeh's long black hair was hanging loosely around her shoulders. The girls, a few of whom I recognised from the beautician's course, were preparing to thread her face and eyebrows. One of the girls was holding a long spool of thread and rotating it around her hand to take off the hair from Fatemeh's face. She squirmed with discomfort but did not otherwise appear unhappy. By the end of this process, Fatemeh's skin was red, almost raw. With her eyebrows shaped her eyes looked larger, sharper. She looked more mature. Then the girls brought out boxes of make-up and creams. They cleansed her skin with alcohol and put on moisturiser, and then began the colourful process.

Fatemeh's make-up was to match her dark pink

dress, waiting on a wire hanger above the door. It was an elaborate dress with sequins and beads. The girls applied shimmery pink, white and gold eye shadow, followed by fake eyelashes with tiny black diamonds on the tips. Fatemeh turned fashionable, up to the minute, by the Kabul beauty standards of March 2009.

We were to have dinner at Hope House first, followed by the henna celebrations at Fatemeh's house. When I walked back, Hope House was bubbling over with happiness. The common room was packed with girls and women dressed in bright colours. Sameera and a few girls were playing the drum, and the older girls were dancing to rhythmic claps. Smaller girls and boys were climbing on Mahboba's shoulders, as someone was putting lipstick on her. She was laughing and gestured to me to join them.

Camera in hand, I got involved in the girls' celebration as they brought tubes of henna and painted each other's hands. Arezoo insisted on painting a design on my hands. The girls continued to dance and sing in the background while she created an elaborate geometric design on the top of my right hand.

While I sat and waited for the henna to dry, I observed the children. Warm, happy, hopeful. It was one of the most blissful moments of the entire trip. It was the moment I knew that in our own small way, Amin and I had made a difference. I hugged the girls as they sat with me, waiting. For the first time, I handed my precious camera to one of the children. She took a picture of me, Arezoo and one of the other girls, Halima. The three of us, sisters, looked into the camera as a couple of young boys squeezed into the top of the frame. Of all my photos from Afghanistan, this is my favourite. Our faces full of joy, sadness and love: all the emotions I experienced during this journey.

After the henna had dried, I headed over to Amin in the boys' rooms. Unlike the gentle procession in the girls' section, the boys were packed into one of the rooms, shouting, screaming and dancing like it was a concert of some imaginary music. It was rowdy, full of life. They had been given a free pass to anything and everything for the night.

In another room, I found the groom dressed in a shiny silver suit with a huge yellow tie and a light purple shirt. As I entered, Amin was filming them putting henna on his feet. With one sock on and his foot stretched out, Abdul Fattah went red when he saw me. 'Khanoom Sanaz!' he called out and laughed quietly. What they were doing had no resemblance to the girls' paintings. Their design was coming out as thick blobs and unsightly shapes.

As the evening wore on, the celebrations continued at Fatemeh's house, where she was waiting for the party to arrive.

All of Hope House came together to accompany the groom to the bride's house. The girls had prepared candles on plates covered with gold and silver tinsel to light the way through the dark valley. Candles glittering like fireflies, the party headed with song and drums across to Fatemeh's house.

We had just left Hope House when a taxi pulled up with Abdul Fattah's enigmatic mother, his older brother and his sister, who had all come from Takhar. He greeted his estranged family with hugs and kisses. It had been years since they had seen each other. Takhar is some four hundred kilometres away and the journey is not an easy one to make. Arm in arm, reunited, they continued the candle-lit procession. Nearly a hundred people packed into Fatemeh's room. Fatemeh was standing in a corner with some of the girls. In her sparkling pink dress, she was slouching and holding one arm across her chest, with the other covering her smile. She didn't look anyone directly in the eye; her gaze only rested sometimes on her friends as people danced in front her.

The henna was brought on a many-tiered tray decorated with plastic flowers. Girls took turns dancing with the tray to the drum beats accompanied by songs and claps. At one point, I found myself with Amin, in the middle of the crowd, dancing with the tray.

When Mahboba took the tray, it was time to move on. She took some henna and put it in Fatemeh's palm. A piece of white cloth, symbolic of her virginity and purity, was wrapped around her hand. The dancing continued until the henna dried. Abdul Fattah stood next to Fatemeh, holding her other hand. He whispered into her ear occasionally and she giggled.

Nik Mohammad occasionally stuck his head into the room to take a darting supervisory look around. He didn't take part in the event.

The celebrations continued until the children had

eaten too many sweets and everyone had danced to the point of exhaustion. When the younger ones had fallen asleep and had to be carried by the older children to their beds at Hope House, we knew it was time to get in the van and head to the cousin's house.

As I drifted into sleep, Panjshir Valley felt like a lifetime ago. The next day was the day we had been waiting for this entire trip. But no one could have anticipated the turn of events that would take place.

36

On the day of the wedding, before the rest of us were up, Mahboba headed out to the baths and then on to a beauty salon with some of the women. Virginia, Pari and I were to be dropped off at Hope House, and Amin was to go with Abdul Fattah and Seddiq to the markets to pick up Abdul Fattah's suit and book a wedding hall for the party later that night.

I was no stranger to Afghan weddings. In July 2006, we had found ourselves invited to an exuberant one. One afternoon at Aina, as we were chatting to Reza, one of the boys had turned up in a suit and tie. He was heading to a friend's wedding and invited Amin and me to come with him. Naturally, we agreed.

We were introduced to the family and even though no one knew us, they welcomed us wholeheartedly. Amin was taken to the men's area and I to the women's. There looked to be about five hundred women in my section, and an equally large group in the men's.

When I arrived, the bride and groom were sitting in a corner of the hall. She wore an elaborate beaded green outfit, with bright make-up that matched her dress and he, the only man in the women's section, kept his head low, gazing at the table in front of him. I was greeted warmly by the couple and offered a plate of sweets and some fruit. Women in beaded and lace gowns were dancing in the centre of the room to the sound of hand drums. Although my stay was short, it had been enough for me to get a taste of an expensive modern Afghan wedding.

In recent years, weddings had become big business in Afghanistan. From make-up artists to halls, car hire companies, musicians, catering and photography, those involved in the industry, inspired by foreign influences, were feeding the need of Afghans to celebrate their weddings at a certain standard – and price. A wedding in Kabul can set the groom back between twenty thousand and eighty thousand US dollars, depending on how elaborately the couple wants to celebrate. The hire of a rare limousine can come to two thousand US dollars per night, and some delicacy dishes can cost as much as a hundred US dollars per head. In a country where people are obliged to invite hundreds, it adds up astronomically. Of course, these lavish affairs are not for everyone. The people who go the extra length are often business people, some of those who have lived elsewhere and returned to Afghanistan after the Taliban, starting much needed infrastructures and businesses. There are options for those with not such deep pockets. But even those can cost in the thousands of dollars.

The wedding of Abdul Fattah and Fatemeh, however, was not going to be anything fancy. For a start, most of the cost was covered in-house. The dress was designed and sewn at the Sewing Centre; the beautician graduates were to do the make-up; and we were doing the film and photography. They were not going to decorate the place with flowers, hire a limousine or even a car for that matter – the default mode of transport was the school bus with

Chinese writing on it – and Seddiq had some power to negotiate the hall price because it was an affair for orphans.

Theirs was to be a modest and simple event. It could not have been any other way, given they didn't even have a hall booked until the morning of the ceremony, where wedding venues were in high demand and booked months in advance. In our three visits to Kabul between 2006 and 2009 I had witnessed how these halls, with names like 'Pearl', 'Ocean', 'Beauty' and 'Love', had popped up all over the city. These purpose-built structures, decorated with statues of sphinxes, eagles and lions on green, red or even pink walls and pillars, towered in the bland dusty landscape of Kabul. They were unmissable; at night they lit up with extravagant lighting like a mini Vegas strip after the power went out for the rest of the city. These halls seemed to be serving customers every night, something we saw on our drive to Mahboba's cousin's house. To find one that was available on the same night – and at the right price – was going to be a challenge, and Seddiq already knew this before he set out.

On the morning of Abdul Fattah and Fatemeh's wedding, Hope House was transformed. The air was fragrant with the children's clean clothes and cheap perfume. The older girls were taking care of the younger ones, while doing their own hair and make-up and selecting clothes and shoes.

Some girls had taken Fatemeh to the baths. Then she was to go home where the graduate beauticians would do her make-up and hair. Her green lace dress was already hanging on the window inside the Sewing Centre, next to a white one that they had borrowed. The plan was to gather in the evening at Fatemeh's house where they would do the formal and religious part of the ceremony. Then we would all head to the wedding hall for the party.

All morning, Pari was kept busy in the office, and Virginia was writing. I floated around and filmed at Hope House with the camera Amin had left behind. At noon Maryam brought us lunch. We had just sat down when Obeid, one of the men who worked in the office, went running to the entrance of Hope House. By the gate stood several armed policemen. We observed the conversation from a distance. When he came back, he was on the phone, fuming.

It turned out that Nik Mohammad had called the police. He had told them that we had kidnapped his daughter and taken her to the baths, and were planning on a wedding in the hall without his consent. He demanded to see his daughter married straight away in his house or he would not let the wedding proceed. The police, who could not make any sense of all this, had come to enquire. When Obeid explained, they said that there wasn't much they could do legally. Nik Mohammad had no case, but given his state of mind the best option would be to accept what he wanted or else he could ruin everything.

Abdul Fattah arrived, red in the face, less than ten minutes later. He called Seddiq and Mahboba but couldn't get through. The police were still standing by, telling him that the best thing to do would be to go right away and perform the religious part of the ceremony so that at least Nik Mohammad would leave them alone. By signing the papers, he was handing over the responsibility for his daughter to Abdul Fattah. After this, he could not bother them anymore because she was legally not in his charge. Abdul Fattah wanted, at least out of respect for all their hard work, for Mother Mahboba and Seddiq to be there for the signing of the documents. The police suggested that if we waited, Nik Mohammad might decide that he didn't want the marriage to happen, even though he had already taken the money.

Obeid and Abdul Fattah decided to head over to Fatemeh's house. Abdul Fattah disappeared for a few minutes and came back in the neon silver suit he had worn the night before. I picked up the camera and followed them. The policemen in their green uniforms with guns hanging off their shoulders, Abdul Fattah in his shiny silver suit and purple tie and Obeid in his Afghan clothes all walked across the dusty valley and into Fatemeh's house for a wedding ceremony.

The men sat in the room to the left. I was guided to Fatemeh's room, where she was still getting ready. She was in the green dress. One of her hands already had glue-on red nails, and the other did not. She had her full make-up on, with green shimmery eye shadow that matched her outfit, except she still had no lipstick. She was about to cry. I stood in the doorway where I could easily manoeuvre between the two spaces. I filmed her getting ready while in the other room the men were preparing the documents.

In the men's space, an Imam was already present, alongside the policemen, Fatemeh's phantom good-boy brother, whom I recognised from photographs, and Nik Mohammad. Abdul Fattah was seated next to Fatemeh's brother. When the brother went around the room offering sweets, Abdul Fattah didn't take any. Fatemeh's brother left one by his foot. The documents took some time to prepare, and the girls were taking this opportunity to make Fatemeh as ready as possible.

The Imam began the ceremony. He read a few lines from the Qur'an and asked Abdul Fattah if he would take Fatemeh to be his wife. He had to ask three times, as part of the tradition. Abdul Fattah responded three times that he did.

Then Obeid moved to Fatemeh's room. The girls held up a large green sheet to keep the distance between Fatemeh and him. In Islamic tradition, a male member of the family usually represents and relays the girl's decision to the Imam. Obeid asked Fatemeh who she wanted to represent her. Fatemeh did not say her father or her brother, she said instead Seddiq. When Obeid told her Seddiq was not here,

Fatemeh teared up. Obeid suggested her brother. She nodded behind the curtain and the girls echoed her agreement. Papers were signed and given to Fatemeh. She signed them and held onto the documents with both hands, one with nail polish and the other still white, tears falling onto the paper.

The moment we had all been waiting for was finally over. But there was no celebration, no happiness, no dancing. The men in the next room ate fruit and the girls carelessly finished polishing Fatemeh's fake nails.

And with this, they were married. Just like that.

37

The policemen picked up the guns they had rested against the wall and left after the papers were signed. Some blush and lipstick were hastily put on Fatemeh's frowning face. Her head was wrapped with a green scarf as she was ushered out of her father's house for the first time free from his authority, and into the dilapidated Chinese minibus to be driven across the valley to Hope House.

I ran after them barefoot as I couldn't find my shoes, and jumped into the bus filming. The bride and groom sat, with big frowns, while the girls began to sing and dance in the minutes it took us to cross the valley. Dozens of the younger children, dressed for the party, ran excitedly to welcome the newlyweds.

Some of the smaller girls wore wedding gowns, christening dresses anywhere else, donated perhaps by someone in Australia. The dresses were too short for some, so they wore them on top of jeans. These girls were the most excited, shouting and screaming at the sight of Fatemeh.

I wondered what the fantasy of a wedding was like for these children. To this day, every time I watch the film I find it an ironic and touching moment of happiness and despair. These little girls, who were excitedly chasing the bus, dreamed of being a bride one day. But did they know what it meant for them to be a bride in Afghanistan? Did they know of the joy, sadness, horror and fear that lay before and after the one night they would look their best? This moment always reflects that duality for me. As they ran with their dreams, Fatemeh, the bride, sat in despair over events she had no control of.

As a group of jubilant girls and boys accompanied the bride and groom to the common room, Mahboba arrived. She was wearing a beaded white Afghan dress and she'd had her make-up done: her eyes were wider, her skin clearer. But even this could not hide her disbelief. She found her way through the children to Abdul Fattah. When he whispered something in her ear, she left and headed downstairs to the office.

Obeid was in the office when Mahboba came in. He explained what had happened. Mahboba was recounting this to Virginia when Seddiq arrived with Amin, bright red.

'What's going on?' Mahboba asked Seddiq as he passed Virginia and sat behind his desk. 'Did you book the hall?'

'Yes. I did.'

'Good, let's go then.'

'No, we are not going,' he said.

'What do you mean, we are not going?'

'I don't want to go to the hall. We have put so much effort into this. I cannot deal with this anymore. Why should we go there? We have the girl here.'

'Seddiq, come on. Don't let one crazy man ruin everything. Think about the happiness of the children. You paid for the hall already. We will lose our money and you will ruin our film.'

'I don't care if we lose money now. And I don't care about the film. I'm fed up.' He got up to go. 'And please don't disturb me. I don't want to be disturbed.'

Mahboba, Virginia and I watched as he left.

'What do we do now?' Virginia asked.

'We are going to the hall. I am not going to let this ruin the happiness of the children,' Mahboba said.

'How are we going to do that, if he doesn't want to go?' Virginia asked.

'I'll make him go. Give him some time. You guys go and change,' Mahboba said, her voice unwavering.

We changed into our outfits and joined everyone upstairs. In the midst of the festivities, Abdul Fattah came to Mahboba and whispered in her ear. As he had to rush back, he had forgotten to pick up his suit for the night. I followed Mahboba as she left for the office. There she found Jameel and told him to pick up the suit. Then she looked for Seddiq. When she couldn't find him, she called him.

'Please, take a shower and get dressed so we can go to the hall. Everyone is waiting for you. You are being childish.' She paused to listen to him.

'Listen, Seddiq. Listen, I don't care what he has done. It is not about him. It is about the children, Abdul Fattah and Fatemeh.'

Then there was a long silence.

'I don't care. Get dressed and come down here. We are leaving soon. Your attitude is boring me.'

She hung up and went out to tell everyone to get ready.

Ten minutes later, the children were lining up and waiting to go.

The hall that Seddiq had managed to secure had no big Roman columns or fancy chandeliers. The men's and women's sections were haphazardly separated by large digital prints of various abstract shapes and colours. A group of us arrived earlier than the children to set up. Seddiq had also hired an all-male traditional band, and they were already tuning their instruments.

Over several trips the minibus transported the children to the hall. They danced to the live music on their way in. Some younger girls wore tiny tiaras. The older girls had perfect hair, and wore their make-up self-consciously. They piled into the hall and sat at the round tables that had been dressed with white tablecloths and chairs with big ribbons on their backs. The younger boys sat at a table of their own in the women's quarter. Some got up on the dance floor before the music had really started and practised their taekwondo moves. The servers brought out a large three-tiered cake made with green and white icing to match Fatemeh's dress, and placed it on a table decorated with plastic flowers.

Some time later the bride and groom arrived in the minibus. We rushed upstairs to document this long-awaited moment. We caught them as they were coming through the entrance to the hall. Self-conscious, they stared down and slowly descended the stairs. Claps, cheers and loud whistles welcomed them. For the first time that day, a faint trace of a smile appeared on Fatemeh's lips. The band continued to play as the couple walked towards the platform.

And then the festivities began. Young boys and girls were already exhausting themselves on the dance floor. The older girls, more reserved, jumped up occasionally, dancing to some of the songs they liked.

Not long after, Seddiq showed up. Dressed up and happy, he greeted everyone. His arrival was the cause of a real smile for the bride and groom.

Halfway through the ceremony, the couple headed to a back room where they changed their outfits. Abdul Fattah now wore his dark suit, brought by

Jameel, and Fatemeh was helped into the borrowed white dress.

Pari, Virginia and I used this opportunity to take some posed wedding photographs. Fatemeh had never had her photo taken; she had no idea what to do. We had to instruct. 'Put your hand on his shoulder,' we said. She blushed and looked down. 'Look into the camera.' She looked to the side. 'Smile.' She put her hand on her face. It came down to Amin to soften up the couple, cracking jokes about the music, the darkness of the room, their clothes, his own beard, and anything he could think of to get Fatemeh to smile. When she did, I managed to get some happy portraits of the two.

It was only then, in seeing Abdul Fattah and Fatemeh smile, that I realised we finally had a wedding. It was a moment of disbelief, the moment when I felt we had made a change.

Several weeks before, Fatemeh had been at risk of being given away to an old man, but now here she was, smiling and posing on her wedding night with the young man she loved. I went to Mahboba to express my gratitude and joy, with my heart feeling warm and my eyes brimming. Amin followed me.

She was standing with Pari and Virginia. When we came together, in this moment, I broke down and the others, seeing me, joined in. We all held each other close, overcome with elation and relief at last.

38

The day after the wedding, Hope House felt different. A sense of calm enveloped the grounds.

The couple had finally achieved their dream, but at a cost. When we accompanied them back to Hope House after the ceremony, both Abdul Fattah and Fatemeh had looked stricken. What Nik Mohammad had done was a dishonour they could not forget. On the way back, Abdul Fattah had decided that he wouldn't stay at Nik Mohammad's. He had arranged for someone to take all of their belongings from Nik Mohammad's house to the room in the half-built house where we had stayed the first few nights. They had set themselves up there. We decided to visit them.

So innocent were the couple that when we knocked Fatemeh ran and hid behind the curtains. Abdul Fattah was blushing ear to ear when he opened the door. We did not want to disturb their first morning as husband and wife and left after a quick greeting. Mahboba stayed on to chat to them about their first night together.

We returned to find Virginia sitting by herself on a small platform in the middle of the garden, reading over her journal entries. She was leaving the next day. Safely. Her voice quavered as she told us how wrong she had been about everything she had thought about Afghanistan, and how, even now, she still didn't understand anything. This country was an enigma to the outside world, with customs that sometimes made little sense from our perspectives. But we had to accept the way things worked, and the way people lived. We sat there in silence, reflecting.

We spent the rest of the day lazily playing with the children. There was suddenly nothing else to do. There was no need to rush or make anything happen, except enjoy the company of the children.

Virginia left the following afternoon. The

children gathered to say goodbye, with brave faces. Her departure was a reminder for me. We would be leaving in two days on the weekly flight to Mashhad. We spent the rest of our time with the children, playing chase and hopscotch, giving them piggybacks from one end of the garden to the other. The youngest crawled on us, and Amin, Pari and I carried them on our backs. At one point Amin balanced four boys on his arms, shoulder and back. We laughed until our bellies ached. Below the laughter and joy there was sadness, and so many mixed emotions.

Throwing ourselves wholeheartedly into play, we were trying to stop time. During our stay we had tried, unsuccessfully, not to get attached; we knew it would feel impossible to leave. We also hadn't wanted to give the children a false sense of comfort that we could not offer permanently. We didn't know if we would ever see them again or even if some would grow up, and all they would recall of us would be vague memories. But for those few hours, all we wanted to do was to immerse ourselves in the moment to forget how soon we'd have to say goodbye.

When the time came to depart, the children

gathered around us. Arezoo, visibly emotional, ran inside. Halimeh followed. The smaller children were clinging onto our hands and belongings. Heywat, a boy of four or five, came up to me, opened my palm and gave me a toy, a tiny race car. It was a McDonald's gift, probably given to some kid in Australia with a Happy Meal and then discarded. It had somehow landed in his hands, and now in mine. It was a beaten-up toy, but I am sure that for Heywat it was one of the more precious of his few belongings. To this day, I keep it next to my most valuable possessions on my altar to remind me of another reality that exists in this world.

After a tearful goodbye with long hugs, we got into the van. It was good to know that the people who had come so suddenly into the children's lives were not all leaving as suddenly as they had come. Pari still had one more week and Mahboba had managed to extend her stay for another two.

Or maybe I was tricking myself into thinking that the children would not be alone after we left. Deep down I knew the reality. Unlike our last two trips, the busyness of Hope House and the rush to make the film had left me with no time for reflection. Now the emotions came all at once. We had, despite all odds, managed to make this film and change the lives of the people involved. I had come to love the children. In the month that we had spent with them, they had become my family. I had come to know almost every child by name, I knew their backgrounds and the trauma they carried in their bodies. I felt like I, too, had become part of the Hope House family and it was so very hard to leave them.

39

When we arrived at the airport, Amin and I were separated for physical pat-downs. I was given a tokenistic check in a shipping container which doubled as the security women's bedroom. A kettle was boiling on a small gas cylinder next to a bed, suitcases were stashed to the side. The security women always looked alike: slightly overweight and wearing lots of make-up. To ease their boredom they liked to stall you by chatting about where you were going and where you were coming from. When I told a security woman I was going to Iran, she was surprised. 'The flight has departed already.'

'I don't think so. It is only twelve and we are not meant to fly out until two.'

'Well, I don't know then.' She patted me down over my clothes, under which I could have hidden any number of large and dangerous things.

The departure hall appeared deserted, as if the airport was closed. When we searched for the check-in counter for Mahan Air, we found it empty. We asked one of the men at the other counter. He told us the flight was about to depart. It was not even twelve-thirty.

'What do you mean?'

'Hold on.' He paged someone.

A stout man ran from the other side of the airport, huffing and puffing. 'Where have you been?' It was the Kabul representative of Mahan Air. We had seen him two weeks earlier at the Mahan office when we had confirmed our tickets. He oversaw the entire one-flight operation from Kabul to Tehran every week.

'Hurry up. You are late.'

We were confused. 'What do you mean we are late?'

'The flight is about to depart.'

'But it's only twelve-thirty,' Amin said. 'It is scheduled for two.'

'Yes, but the people were here except you two, and there was a clear runway time at one, so we boarded everyone.' We could not believe our ears. He was scolding us for being late?

But this wasn't a total surprise. My father had missed a flight in a similar way when working in Kabul. Even though he turned up two hours before, they had already left on a clear runway.

With our luggage in tow, we ran after the sweating, huffing man. The security guards asked us to put our luggage into the scanner, but no one even looked at the screen. The Mahan Air representative grabbed our bags and told us to run. We sprinted up to the second floor to get our passports stamped. Usually this area was full of people, but now it was empty. Only one man sat behind the counter. He took his time flipping through every page, asking us questions before casually stamping our passports.

With the Mahan Air representative waiting for us at the end of the corridor, we headed out onto the tarmac, where our plane was waiting. He ran ahead and motioned us to hurry. The engines were running. They were rolling steps towards the plane so we could board. They didn't even put our bags into the belly of the plane, but stored them somewhere at the front of the cabin. The plane was packed, with only two empty seats. Everyone was eyeing us, blaming us for delaying the flight. We had not even sat down properly when the plane started to taxi. It took off while we were still buckling up.

I had expected this departure to be more romantic, with a bit more closure. As I looked out of the window while the plane ascended, I felt both sadness and relief. There was a sorrow about the lives of the people that I was leaving behind, and a feeling of being helpless about changing anything for the better. There was also deep affection for the children; I was already missing them. But there was relief that came from knowing that we had actually shot the film, we were returning home safe, and that at the end of this trip would be a proper bathroom, a hot shower and fresh clothes. Still, my heart ached for those who continued to live in Afghanistan never knowing such luxuries, or even the basic necessities.

The Mashhad airport seemed pristine after a month in Kabul. There was not a speck of dust or mud anywhere. When I went to the bathroom, after a month of holes in the ground, the porcelain sink and toilet bowl seemed like something out of Hong Kong's Shangri-La Hotel.

When we reached the domestic terminal, we were asked to put our bags under the scanner. For some reason, Amin refused.

To this day, I don't understand why.

He told the teenager behind the counter, a provincial rookie doing his army training, that he was afraid the films in the bag would be damaged.

'What? Film? How many films?' His eyes widened.

'A hundred and twenty.'

'Whaaat?' He stood up. 'What kind of tapes do you have?'

'Tapes for a film from Afghanistan.'

'I cannot let you go through, sir. I need to talk to my supervisor.' The boy looked around. He had never encountered anything like this because the entry of tapes, films and other recorded material into Iran is strictly controlled, to ensure that they abide by the law of the Islamic regime and are up to moral standards.

'What do you mean? There is no need for that. I will show you,' Amin said, about to open his bag.

'These are just tapes from a documentary film we made in Kabul about children in an orphanage.'

'Okay. But I have to tell my supervisor about it.'

'Listen. No need for that. I will put it under the scanner. No problem.' He grabbed his bag.

'I can't let you do that now.' The boy pulled the bag back.

'If I had not told you, you wouldn't even have known.' Amin glared at him with one hand on the bag.

'But now I know and I can't just let you go,' he said as he pulled the bag closer to him on the table.

The supervisor, watching this push and pull from a distance, approached us. 'What's the problem here?'

When Amin told him that he had a hundred and twenty tapes, he said, 'We can't let you take them. A few weeks ago, a filmmaker had one tape, one tape, and we confiscated it.'

'Why?'

'Because we need to check the content to make sure there is nothing inappropriate.'

'I can assure you there is nothing inappropriate. Look at us. This is my wife,' he said pointing to me, 'and we have just spent one month in the dirt and mud of Kabul to make a documentary about widows and orphans. All we want to do now is to go home and make this film. I am telling you,' Amin said, raising his voice a notch, 'there is nothing inappropriate in these films.'

The man looked around. 'Okay. Calm down. No need to make a scene. Can I please have your passport?'

As the man glanced at the passport, Amin motioned to me and said out loud that I should go and check in at the domestic counter. I began to walk away very slowly.

The man asked Amin, 'Do you work for any organisations? Are you media? Are you a reporter?'

I don't know what inspired him to do this but Amin took out his father's old press pass, which he carried around as a memento. His father had worked for an Iranian media organisation some fifteen or twenty years before. The card bore a picture of him with a beard, which looked nothing like Amin. It had expired over ten years ago.

'Yes,' Amin said as he confidently handed the card over to the man.

My heart skipped a beat. I froze where I was. I

had no idea what Amin's strategy was, or even if he had one. The man looked at the card and looked at Amin and said, 'Are you Mr Nasser Palangi?'

'Of course I am,' he said confidently.

I could not believe my ears. I watched, in awe, wondering how Amin was going to work his way out of this one, considering we had less than an hour to the departure of our domestic leg.

'Okay, Mr Palangi. Give me a few minutes. Let me call my supervisor.' He went into a room, taking the card and the passport with him.

My heart was beating so fast that I began to sweat. Amin looked relatively calm. I was worried that they would either take the films or imprison him for lying. Or both.

The man invited Amin into his room. This time, I followed. Amin didn't object so I sat down beside him on a sofa. The man sat behind his desk and made a call. He explained the situation, with both the card and the passport in front of him all the while. Fortunately, the passport remained closed.

'Yes, sir,' he would say occasionally. 'I understand. Yes.'

He hung up and turned to Amin. 'Dear brother,

I am sorry to say that my boss told me that the films need to be confiscated and sent to Tehran, where they will be checked by the ministry to make sure their contents are safe and clean.'

'Listen, brother,' Amin said, 'I am not leaving these films here. There is no way I am leaving these films here. My wife and I, we have just spent one month of our lives making a film about widows and orphans. What kind of content do you think we have there?'

'I am sorry but these are the rules.'

'I understand that. But I have to get these films edited and your process could damage the film. It could take months!'

'I am sorry but you have to leave the films.'

'If I had not told you, I could have just walked out of here. This is what one gets for being honest in this country. We just have to learn to lie. This is what you want.'

The man suddenly seemed a bit taken a back. 'I understand your concern.' He paused. 'Okay, tell me – what is the content of the films?'

'They are interviews and some shots of children playing.'

'Why do you have so many films then?'

'Because we were there for one month.'

'What kinds of things do they talk about?'

'Their everyday life, the difficulties of life in the country. The poverty, the sadness.'

The man actually seemed to be considering this as he leaned back in his chair and played with his chin. 'So can you show me some of the footage, then?'

'Of course,' Amin said confidently.

I shuffled in my seat. Most of the footage had been filmed on the camera that Mahboba had brought. Although the films looked identical, the formats were different. Mahboba was to take the camera back with her to Sydney, and we had only the small camera. Fortunately, Amin knew exactly which films had been shot on the small camera.

The footage he played back was of the shoeshine boy's mother. She was saying how her child wanted to go to school.

'Fast-forward, please.'

Now the footage was of some children playing in the mud.

'Okay,' the man said. 'Play another one.'

Amin looked through the films and found the

right one. The man noticed that he was looking for a specific one and asked, 'What are you looking for? Just pick one at random.'

Amin explained to him that our camera could not read all of the tapes.

'Show me anyway,' he said, and randomly picked one. 'This one.'

'Okay.' Amin put it in the camera. It was all black.

'Fast-forward,' he demanded. Still black. 'Show me this.' He picked up another one. Amin played it and it was the same thing.

'Okay.' He leaned back. 'Give me some time. I need to discuss this. Please wait outside.'

He closed the door to his glass office. We watched as he spoke on the phone for a good five minutes. Occasionally he would look at the ID card he was holding. By then we had less than half an hour to get to our next flight.

He hung up and motioned us in. 'I had a chat with my boss. He insists that we keep the films and check them.'

The next strategy was to start begging. I finally spoke up. 'Dear sir,' I said, 'look at us. We are working for a charity. I am sure you can find a way to write this one off. You have seen it. That is all it is. Children and widows.'

'I understand, sister,' he said. He seemed to be considering something as I spoke.

'We have a connecting flight soon. If we miss this, we will have to spend the day here and our families will be worried and waiting for us,' I continued.

'Okay.' He sighed and turned to Amin. 'You are like my son.' He had obviously not noticed the date of birth on the ID card. 'I see you are both very hardworking. I am going to ask you to look into my eyes and promise me that there is nothing inappropriate in these films.'

'I promise you, sir,' Amin said.

'Are you sure?' he asked again.

'Definitely. All you saw is all it is. There is nothing more to it.'

'All right.' He held out his hand to shake Amin's and looked him deeply in the eye. 'I have no choice but to accept your word on this. It is now on your conscience, young man, if you have inappropriate material.'

'You can rest assured that I don't, sir.'

'Okay, then.' He slid the identity card into the

passport and gave it back to Amin.

'Have a safe trip and good luck with the film.'

'Thank you, sir,' I said. We rushed out of the office and over to the domestic terminal. At a second set of scanners, Amin just put the films through and no one even flinched. We picked up the bag and made our plane a few minutes before departure.

We arrived in Tehran exhausted, dirty, and still unsettled by what had happened in Mashhad.

My parents were to pick us up from the airport. But only my father was waiting at the arrivals gate. We were surprised. I asked where my mother was. 'A friend invited her over to dinner, so she went there,' he said.

My mother, who had insisted on me not going, who had always made an effort to come to the airport no matter where I was returning from, was not the type who would go to a dinner instead. Maybe she was still angry with me.

When we arrived at the complex where my parents lived, my mother's car was in the carport.

'Where's my mother?'

'Let's go upstairs first.'

'What do you mean?' We were heading into the elevator. 'Tell me what's going on. Is she dead?'

'The thing is…' My father paused.

I was sure that my mother must have died of the grief I had caused her by going to Afghanistan. I couldn't hold back the tears.

'Listen,' he said. 'Listen. She is okay.'

'What do you mean?'

'She is okay. She is in hospital. But she is fine.'

By now we had reached the apartment and he was opening the door.

'Why is she in hospital? I want to talk to her now. If she is okay, let me talk to her. Now. I want to go and see her.' I wiped my face and turned to Amin. 'Did you know about this?'

He shook his head.

'Then let me talk to her right now,' I demanded. 'Right now.'

'Okay.' My father called her and she picked up. I started sobbing. 'Where are you? What is going on? Are you okay? You scared me. Where are you? I want to come and see you.'

'I am all right. I am okay, don't worry,' she said. 'I can't talk because there is someone else in my room who is sleeping. Ask your father to explain.'

A few days after we left, my mother had started complaining about chest pain and breathlessness. Although she had no history of heart disease, my sister had insisted she have it checked. Initially the doctors thought nothing of it. Just stress, they said. But the test results showed that two of her main arteries were almost completely blocked, with a third fifty per cent blocked. The doctors said that if she had come in a week later, she would have been in serious trouble. They suggested an angiography as soon as possible, a quick and straightforward procedure.

When my mother went in, she had to wait for nearly twelve hours. The doctor had been operating and seeing other patients and got to her at around four o'clock the next morning, exhausted. While putting the catheter into her artery, he punctured its wall. When we returned from Afghanistan, she had just had surgery to repair the damage.

I had fantasised about standing under hot running water. But I didn't care about that now. I took a two-minute shower and demanded to go and see my mother. At the hospital, I begged the night nurses to let me in. It was close to midnight and most other patients had been asleep for hours. They brought her out in a wheelchair.

It was one of the most devastating moments in my life.

I had just come back from a place where countless young children had experienced the grief of losing a parent. In the time between finding out what happened to my mother and seeing her, I felt this grief approaching, ready to engulf me too. Although I couldn't even imagine what they felt, this brought me closer to the children I had just left behind.

After this flood of emotion, being able to touch my mother, alive and present, I was deeply grateful. Here was my family who, despite everything, still loved me unconditionally. The tears that were flowing again came with a feeling of solace, contentment.

That night a slight discomfort that I was feeling in my throat started to accumulate into something more. I took a cold tablet and went to bed. The entire journey seemed like a dream now. My head was spinning as I closed my eyes. Would the things that had emerged in the dream continue growing? Would they bear fruit and make a difference?

On the verge of falling asleep, I could only hope this dream would become an answer of sorts to the one from my teenage years, that of the field with all the children asking me to help.

Epilogue

About a month after we returned to Australia, Virginia's story for the *7.30 Report* aired nationally. A touching glimpse into Mahboba's activities and projects, the clip raised sixty thousand Australian dollars overnight.

Pari, Virginia and I collectively exhibited our photos, once at an event for Mahboba's Promise where we sold all our prints, and again at an event in Canberra organised by Virginia. Pari continued to work on her photography project with the children and raised awareness through their exhibition. Virginia continued to be a speaker and advocate of Mahboba's Promise, recounting her experiences wherever she could.

I made a gift for the children at Hope House. I

printed some four hundred of their portraits and gave them to Mahboba to send to Kabul with whoever was going next. I also made an album of the wedding portraits of Abdul Fattah and Fatemeh.

But the main project grew slowly. It took Amin and me five years to transform nearly a hundred and eighty hours of footage into a film and release it. At first, Amin and I tried to edit the footage ourselves. With his work and my PhD and other things in daily life, our many attempts took two years. We also tried to find a producer and a broadcaster for the film but no one in Australia was interested. Even though Mahboba and Virginia were both Australians, the media didn't see the concept as Australian enough, and major TV channels rejected our proposals.

In the meantime, Abdul Fattah and Fatemeh had a baby boy. Mahboba sent us a picture of him: a tiny frail baby wrapped in green, with his eyes and eyebrows pencilled with kohl. Sadly, soon after, he died. During the particularly cold winter of 2011, Fatemeh had taken him to the doctor and on the way back he had caught a cold and died. When Mahboba called and told me this, I was driving. I pulled over and wept as if I had lost a family member.

The little boy's death gave us more drive to keep working on the film but, still, no one was interested. And we couldn't do it on our own.

It wasn't until 2013, when we had managed to gain the interest of Pat Fiske, a teacher at the Australian Film, Televison and Radio School and one of Australia's top producers, that the project started to mature. With Pat on board, we received a post-production grant from Screen Australia to finish the film, which we titled *Love Marriage in Kabul.* Once we had a rough cut, we decided that we needed one more short shoot in Kabul, to get footage that would help us pull the film together.

In December 2013, four years after we had stayed with the children at Hope House, we returned for a quick visit. The city had changed almost beyond recognition but the children made us feel like we had returned home. Hope House was run down. Its white and blue exterior needed a fresh coat of paint. The rooms, too, needed some renovation. But where there had once been a desolate yard was now the permaculture garden with vegetables and fruit.

Most of the children at Hope House were still there and remembered us, and I remembered everyone by name. Some had moved on. Monireh had finished her studies and become a teacher in a remote village. Halimeh was engaged. Arezoo was still at Hope House, but less shy, more refined and elegant. Maryam was now engaged to Nour Agha, one of the boys at Hope House. When we had first met him he was a big boy with glasses, but now he had transformed into a handsome young man studying at university. The boys, now that they were hitting puberty, were much more gentle in their actions and manners than in their pre-teen years.

Some of the women who came to Hope House to receive rations recognised us from four years before. They asked me and Amin if we had any children yet, and the answer shocked them. They thought there was something wrong with us. Something was wrong: we were at the beginnings of a crack in our relationship that eventually led to our separation.

We also returned to the Panjshir Valley. We visited the school; like Hope House, it seemed to need some renovations. Mahboba had just built a new centre in the valley. This was a brand new building, modelled after Hope House, housing fifty children.

The Panjshir Valley, however, didn't feel as safe.

During our visit to the new centre, we went up to the roof to see the view. Amin set up his camera near the ledge and filmed the landscape. Minutes later, Mahboba was called down. Oblivious, we kept playing with the children and filming on the roof. When we went down, several armed men were talking to Mahboba. Amin even filmed the conversation. It was only a few minutes into this that we learned that someone had been ready to shoot Amin while we were on the roof. One of the guards had become furious when he saw someone filming, thinking that he was a spy looking into the surrounding houses. He had already aimed and was ready to shoot when the other guard had suggested that perhaps they should investigate before he actually fired. Mahboba was angry and scolded them. The men left, apologetic. The shock of that moment didn't really hit me until we returned to Hope House later that night. We had escaped disaster by a millimetre.

While in Kabul, we also managed to see the young couple again. Abdul Fattah, who was now a proud university student, studying pharmacy, had come to visit us the day we arrived. We felt close to him, even after all that time: he was like a brother. Since we had last seen them, Fatemeh's father had taken off. No one knew where he was. The couple were now living in his house with Fatemeh's younger brothers. Her older brother was still unmarried but didn't live with them. Fatemeh was pregnant again, this time with a girl. She was no longer the shy fifteen-year-old who slouched with her arms across her body. She looked us in the eye, smiled, and carried herself with much more confidence. She was now a grown woman who had experienced motherhood, and the loss of a child. When we returned to Sydney, we heard that she had given birth to little Boshra, who was healthy and beautiful.

As with every time we had been to Kabul, it was very difficult for us to leave. But this time, somehow, felt different. I didn't have the same feelings of helplessness. I didn't feel overwhelmed. I knew that the film would touch people's hearts. And it did. It won audience choice awards in Australia and overseas, and was shortlisted for a Walkley award.

Finally, there was some fruit, a small way to meet our obligation to the children, the widows, and the women of Afghanistan. It had sprouted from seeds sown well before my time, and I hope it may bear seeds that can carry on growing and giving into the future.

Acknowledgement

The writing of this book has been a journey that has spanned what feels like several lifetimes. I am grateful for the friends and family who listened to me talk about this book and supported my mission.

The manuscript has also had several lives of its own, including a few where it nearly didn't make it. Had it not been for the inner knowing that this book is not about me but about the women and children of Afghanistan, I probably would have given up in the early drafts and after a few rejections. I am glad that I persisted and grateful that others saw the message this book conveys and supported it along the way. In particular, I am grateful to the judges of the University of Melbourne's Peter Blazey Fellowship, whose choice reignited in me the drive to continue with this project at a time when I was ready to give up. It was after winning the fellowship that I once again started approaching publishers, including Xavier Hennekinne of Gazebo Books who coincidentally has also published Peter Blazey's memoir. I would like to thank Xavier for his generous reading, and his meticulous and detailed engagement with me in the editing process.

More than anything, I would like to thank the women and children I met in Afghanistan, every one of their stories touched parts of my soul and heart in ways unimaginable; meeting them pushed and expanded my humanity and humility.

May this work give back to them a thousandfold, in this generation and those yet to come.

www.ingramcontent.com/pod-product-compliance
Lightning Source LLC
LaVergne TN
LVHW041101080826
845145LV00007B/1650

* 9 7 8 0 6 4 8 9 0 1 1 0 5 *